# STORIES FROM THE ARCHIVES
## VOLUME 1

## KODY RICHARDSON

**BEYOND**
THE FRAY PUBLISHING

ISBN 13: 978-1-954528-89-5

Beyond The Fray Publishing,
a division of Beyond The Fray, LLC
San Diego, CA

**BEYOND**
THE FRAY PUBLISHING

SINCE 2018

*This book is lovingly dedicated to the memory of Larry Richardson, Chaz Parrott, Patrick Prochaska, Paul, and Agnus Prochaska. Your impact on my life has shaped who I am today. Though you are no longer with us, you will never be forgotten. Until we meet again.*

*To my beloved fiancé, Meghan Innes—your unwavering support and love have made all my achievements possible.*

*And to my fur daughter, Luna, whose boundless sweetness and joy more than make up for her occasional lapses in intelligence.*

# CONTENTS

# INTRODUCTION

Welcome to *Stories From the Archives: Volume I*, a curated collection of the most chilling, haunting, and terrifying tales from the depths of history. If you're holding this book, you're about to embark on a journey through the eerie and unexplained—stories that have both fascinated and frightened audiences on the *Mystery Archives* YouTube channel.

For years, I've shared these unsettling episodes with a dedicated community of viewers who crave the dark allure of the unknown. Now, through this book and the series it begins, I'm reaching out to a broader audience—those who may not have stumbled upon my videos but have an appetite for the mysterious nonetheless.

Each story in this volume has been selected for its ability to linger in the mind long after the final page is turned. These are tales that tap into our deepest fears, drawing from real events and documented hauntings to create a collection that is as educational as it is eerie.

Whether you're a longtime fan or a new reader, I invite you to delve into these stories, to lose yourself in the dark corridors of history, and to join me in exploring the mysteries that refuse to fade into the shadows. Welcome to the archives. Let the haunting begin.

—Kody Richardson
Creator and host of *Mystery Archives*

# CHAPTER 1
## BROWNSVILLE ROAD HOUSE

Hidden deep within the walls of an old home, something ethereal is lurking, watching...

For years, the family who called this place home believes this entity is harmless but they would soon discover this was not the case.

Evil will rise and its tendrils will infect everything they touch.

Will they make it out alive and with their souls intact?

This is the chilling untold story of the demon of Brownsville Road.

---

The story of the Cranmer family starts with Bob, an Army officer, and his wife Lesa, who married in 1980. Shortly after, they began building their family. In 1986, after Bob left the service and took a job with AT&T, the Cranmers settled in New Jersey. However, their hearts remained in Pennsylvania, where they had grown up. When an unexpected opportunity for a transfer arose, the Cranmers eagerly embraced the chance to move back home.

Although having just built a new house in 1987, the couple found themselves shopping for homes in Brentwood, Pennsylvania. While looking at potential buys, Bob came across a home for sale that he never thought he'd be able to live in – an old, historic home from his childhood. This wasn't just any home, however; it was the home that Bob himself grew up seeing almost daily. He had always felt a pull to the home, to what it represented to him – the history, its style and way of living, and its symbol of success.

Bob contacted the sellers and arranged a walkthrough for him and his family. As the Cranmers arrived and began to tour the inside of the house, their son, Bobby Jr. wandered off by himself as the group went into the basement. When they returned, they found the poor young man crying and hyperventilating, as if he had seen a ghost. Thinking that perhaps due to the boy's young age and imagination he had just scared himself in such a big house, Bob and Lesa wrote the behavior off. As they concluded the tour, despite his wife's misgivings about the size and feel of the house – that it gave her the creeps – Bob dismissed her, seeming almost mesmerized by the home. He continued to question the realtor and would ask the question almost no one asks in these situations, is there anything wrong with the house?

Understanding exactly what he was hinting at, the realtor said that nothing was wrong with the house and that Catholic mass had been conducted several times in the living room of the house. The realtor simply moved on with their conversation. Bob found this response to be odd but nonetheless took the reassurance that had been implied. Later, according to Bob, the couple seemed very anxious to move out, almost as if their very lives depended on it.

Thinking initially that they would want to haggle, he submitted a lowball offer to them. To his shock and amazement, they accepted it without any further negotiations. Not only excited to live in the childhood home of his dreams, but to get it at such a good price almost seemed too good to be true to Bob, and perhaps it was.

It was a cold December day in 1988, but the day was filled with warm feelings. The Cranmer family had just closed on the purchase of their new home, a designated historical landmark by Pittsburgh History & Landmarks, and in due time they would travel from New Jersey. Bob, Lesa and their four kids – Jessica who was four, Bobby Jr. who was three, David who was two, and Charles who was just two months old – would move into and begin living in the home on Brownsville Road.

All seemed normal at first, but this calm normalcy would not last. The family began to notice small but bizarre things happening in their old home. Doors began to open on their own, objects began to move and go missing, and faucets would turn by themselves. Many times – even if the family had been out during the evening – when they would leave the home with the lights off, they would return to not only the lights on but, after a quick sweep of the house, every door and window secured. They had no rational explanation for it. Every single light, including those in the basement would be on.

This was enough to make the Cranmers think. Although it was weird, they weren't really scared at that time. Lesa and Bob concluded they had a ghost, thinking it could've been due to the age and history of the house, but they simply considered it to be Casper the Friendly Ghost. They didn't see it as a threat, and believed it was nothing to worry about – or so they thought.

Things weren't always incredibly active, though; soon things calmed down somewhat in the months that followed. The family started to settle into their normal everyday lives. The occasional strange happenings here and there almost became commonplace, but every so often things would pick back up. Alongside the previously mentioned activity, they began to hear mysterious banging noises all throughout their house at all hours of the day and night, as well as disembodied footsteps echoing all around. Although weird, the family ultimately grew to accept these happenings as normal.

Over the years, Bob went into politics and held political office in the 1990s, first as a councilman and then a county commissioner, gaining local notoriety and status in the Western Pennsylvania area. Despite his career achievements, his family was falling apart. Year by year, it seemed as though things became increasingly dysfunctional for the Cranmer family as a whole. Bob and Lesa would fight frequently, all of which contributed to Lesa and two of the children experiencing serious mental health issues that required hospitalization.

During the ensuing chaos that was becoming his family, Bob had the fleeting thought that whatever was in the house had perhaps contributed to the mental distress of his family, but whenever this feeling would come up, he would simply dismiss it.

One night in 2003, his oldest son Bob Jr attacked Bob in his sleep – a vicious and unprovoked attack, as if his son was in the throes of madness. At this time, it was Bob, Lesa, and all of the kids except for Jessica living at the house, along with Bob's elderly aunt. Following the aftermath of this night, the next morning Bob's aunt was found deceased. She died of natural causes in her bed. Thankfully for Bob Jr, all charges were dropped associated with the attack, but this series of unfolding events seemed to break the dam that had been holding back the paranormal within the Cranmer home. As if the levies had been breached, a tidal wave of spiritual energy was unleashed. The following year in 2004, despite her chaotic and scary childhood, Jessica moves back home with her new husband, Tom and son, Colin.

There was an apartment up on the top floor of the house that Bob felt would be a good fit for the young family. He offered to let them live there so they could save money, get everything in order, and eventually buy a house of their own – something that was becoming increasingly more difficult to do. He also felt that it was a good healing opportunity for the family, allowing them all to be united and together once again.

As his daughter and her family moved their things in, Bob took off his coat and went to hang it in the large walk-in closet underneath the main staircase. As he opened the door to the closet, he noticed that the pull chain for the light was wrapped all the way around the fixture. Thinking it was just the usual weirdness and being rather used to the unusual by that point, Bob dismissed it and unwrapped the chain. Being raised Catholic and continuing to be a spiritual man into his adulthood, Bob decided to do something about the activity for the first time.

On a side table near the closet, he had a bible and a rosary. Believing that this would calm things down, he took the rosary beads and tied them to the chain to the light. Upon closing the door and starting to walk away, he heard the clinking of beads. Rushing back to the door, he opened it, only to find the rosary and the chain wrapped completely around the fixture yet again.

Dismissing things at first but now thoroughly alarmed, Bob grabbed his bible, stepped into the closet, and began to pray out loud. He continued to do so for half an hour. During his time in the closet, he couldn't help but notice that he felt a heavy weight upon his body and the sensation of eyes boring a hole into the back of his skull. After half an hour, he finished and left the closet, closing the door behind him.

In the weeks that followed, Jessica and her family began to settle into their new home in the apartment on the third floor. As Tom went to check on his stepson, he opened his door to find a woman standing over Colin. Believing it to be his wife, he called out to her. The woman then turned, took several steps towards him, and then disappeared before his eyes.

Tom wasted no time in protecting the boy. He rushed in, scooped him up, and headed to his and Jessica's room. At the time, Jessica tried to dismiss what Tom had seen. She thought that if she didn't acknowledge it as reality, then it couldn't be real.

Tom rushed down the stairs and consulted Bob immediately. Bob, not wanting to take any chances with this grandson, decided to sleep in the room for the night. After closing the door, turning on the lamp, and taking a seat in a nearby chair, Bob began to pray. After an hour or so of reading scripture, he decided to try and get some sleep. Lying on his grandson's bed, he slowly drifted off.

Sound asleep, he was soon woken up by massive bangs coming from inside the walls near his head. Waking up in a panic at the sound, his eyes darted back and forth, searching for the source. He then felt a sharp, stinging sensation on the side of his neck. Jumping up, he ran over to the mirror in the room and was shocked by what he saw. From underneath the right side of his ear, down his neck, and onto his torso, there were three long and bloody scratch marks, as if something had clawed him. Frightened and unsure of how to deal with the new situation and the emotions he felt himself experiencing, Bob decides to not discuss the matter with his family for the time being, not wanting to concern them.

The following day, Bobby Jr, the oldest son of the family, was in the living room studying for an exam. As he sat on the couch taking notes from his textbook, he suddenly began to feel as if he was being watched. This made him uncomfortable so, deciding to step outside to get some fresh air, he made his way towards the front door. As he got several feet away from the door, he heard something fly past his head with a sharp tone and crash into the wall beside him. Bewildered and glancing down at his feet, he found a CD from a stack near the entertainment center shattered into a dozen fragments. There was no one else in the room. Unsure of what else to do, he quickly headed to the front door and left.

Fearing for the safety of their family, The Cranmers, now at their wits end with the reoccurring supernatural events taking place in their home, decided to contact a catholic priest for help. A man named Father Mike Sylvania was who they spoke with, and he agreed to assist them by going to bless their house. He arrived in due time and the priest began his blessings. In an effort to sanctify the home, Sylvania travelled from level to level, from room to room. He went from the main floor. to the basement, and then to the upstairs.

It was when he headed upstairs that he began to realize just what the family had been dealing with. As he walked up each step, he too began to feel the stare of a thousand eyes upon him, and the hair on the back of his neck stood on end. He knew then that they were dealing with an infestation. Whether it was human spirits or nonhuman, he couldn't discern. He finished his blessings and encouraged the family to persevere. Then he left.

Weeks later, when the rest of her family was out, Jessica found herself alone and asleep in the upstairs apartment. As she lay in her bed with the large moon hanging overhead, its light piercing the windows, she was suddenly ripped out of a dream state. Her eyes opened, but she was unable to move. It was as if she was paralyzed, but completely coherent. Along with being frozen, she suddenly felt as if someone or some*thing* was sitting on her chest. Then she saw it – a large, shadowy figure at the foot of her bed. As it started to climb on top of her, she tried with every fiber of her being to scream, but all that came out was silence.

To her, anyway.

Her mother, who had returned from running errands, heard her screams from the moment she entered the house. Running upstairs, she found her grown daughter almost inconsolable. She was shaking and crying. Whatever it was that was tormenting her had disappeared. However, regardless of age, the love of a mother eventually brought her back to reality.

The family was now beyond worried – petrified is almost an understatement. Their every waking moments were filled with anxiety and dread. They had hoped that word wouldn't get out but, unbeknownst to them, their situation had caught the attention of the bishop of the Catholic church of Pittsburgh, who in response assigned an experienced priest by the name of Ron Lengwin.

Upon reaching out to Bob on behalf of the church, Father Lengwin concluded that based on what Bob had told him, the sound of his voice, and the overall feel of the call, that this case needed to be investigated further – that this family needed help. He gave the Cranmer family two options. One, they could stay and fight and have the backing of the church, or two, they could leave – but it wouldn't be guaranteed that whatever these entities were wouldn't continue to haunt them. As a family, they decided to stay and fight. As preparations were made by the church to send help, the family tried to hold on.

One morning shortly after the phone call, as the family convened in the dining room for breakfast, Bobby Jr came down and sat at the table. As he explained to his mom that he didn't sleep much and that he tossed and turned all night, he started to feel burning on his back. Before Lesa's very eyes, she watched as scratches formed on her son's back like an invisible hand had taken a razor and sliced him. Each one was approximately six inches long. They called for Bob.

He took one look at his son's back and immediately began to panic. He then started checking all of the children's backs. All of the boys had the same three markings. Remembering back to when he was scratched, he asked the children calmly to go and wash their cuts while he spoke to Lesa. He then finally came clean about his own attack.

He discovered that it was not just him and the children who had been physically marked, but his wife who had been nursing her own wound came clean as well. Located on her left shoulder was a bite mark, one that was so deep that it drew blood. In fact, it had continued to bleed underneath her shirt. Upon further analysis, the bite wasn't like that of a human. It was as if whatever the creature was had fangs of some sort.

Refusing to wait, Bob immediately called the priest back.

Later that day, after receiving special permission, Father Mike returned to perform mass inside the Brownsville home. He believed the scratches to be one of several indications that the infestation within the home was demonic rather than human spirits.

Following mass, as Bob and Lesa were sitting at the dinner table to eat together, they received a call from upstairs. Jessica, not wanting to intrude on their time together, asked if Collin could come down; he would like to see his grandpa and grandma. Hearing that it was no problem, Jessica sent him headed downstairs. From the top floor to the second level were three sets of stairs. As the young man descended, headed towards his grandparents, they suddenly heard him shriek.

Bob got to him first and found Colin shaking like a leaf. The poor child was screaming out, "Monster!" and pointing at an open door.

It was at that moment Bob knew that whatever this thing was wasn't going to stop – that in order to keep part of his family safe, he would have to move them out of the house. The feeling was bittersweet. The family had grown to love the house but, at the same time, Jessica was relieved to get her son out of the situation.

However, Bob, Lesa, and their three sons remained.

Several days after Jessica and her family departed the house, Bob returned home from work. Walking through the hallway headed towards the kitchen, he got the sense he was being watched. He stopped dead in his tracks and slowly turned around to face whatever could be there. However, he sees no figure. Instead, he saw streams of what appeared to be blood on the walls – fresh blood leaking down, as if to mimic how the priest had blessed the home using holy water.

Wanting to make sure he wasn't crazy, Bob called out to Bobby Jr. to come and see what he was seeing. The two shared a moment of shock and unease. The walls were indeed bleeding, and it was unlike anything they had ever seen before.

Bob, at the end of his wits, calls the Catholic church. He speaks with Father Lengwin, who tells him that he's about ready to make the recommendation to the bishop to sanction a proper exorcism of the house, but that the family had to endure one more test. He told him that they needed to have an outside, third party, non-religious group come in and document their findings and then turn in those findings to the church. Bob made several calls and arranged for such a group to come out – a paranormal investigation crew that originated out of Penn state.

They arrived in January of 2005. As two members set things up, the main leader – a man named Adam Blai – finished up a tour of the home with Bob. Unbeknownst to Bob, his main job was to perform an informal psyche evaluation on the family to determine that they were of sound mind and not just spinning fantasies. He determined that they indeed were sane.

Upon further inquiry, he asked Bob when things started to get bad – if there was a catalyzing moment or area of the home. Bob, thinking back, immediately thought of the closet. Upon explaining what had taken place and how things had escalated since that day, Adam believed that this demon originated from underneath the stairs, in or near the closet.

Knocking on the wood exterior of the stairs, it sounded hollow. Believing that the origin could potentially be found there, Bob agreed and assisted him with opening it up to look inside. It was no easy task, but the best way was to cut the wall out from inside the closet, so they did.

Among the cobwebs and dust was indeed an open space – a hidden room of sorts. In the center of the room, covered in more dust – as if it had been sealed in – was a strange looking altar. To the side of this altar was an incredibly old piece of paper. Upon further examination, the paper contained drawings, the name of the original owner, as well as the name 'Malich.'

Malich was the last name of one of the original owners of the home. It's also just one letter off from Molich, a demon from the Old Testament most commonly associated with the Canaanites who worshiped this entity and sacrificed children to it.

Adam, wanting to take a moment, wandered off back into the main living room space to breathe. He then suddenly began to see the letters S, A, T, H, I, appear before him out of nowhere. Then something invisible scratched his forehead.

Adam's screams quickly garnered the attention of the rest of the crew who quickly rushed to his aid. They tried to console him, but he was more driven to figure out what the word 'sathi' meant. Running to the home base setup for the investigation, he quickly began searching the internet. What he found bewildered him further; Sathi was the name of a female demon that served under Molich. Her primary function was to encourage women to sacrifice their children to him.

Based off this new information, Bob began searching the history of the home for anything that could be out of sorts and one such piece of history soon caught his eye. Where the property now stood was once the sight of a grizzly native and settler war which took place in the 1790s. One such story was that a woman and her two children had been killed by the tribes near Fort Pitt. Her house was roughly 6 miles from the fort, placing it almost directly where their home was. With all of this death and sorrow,

Bob wasn't surprised that a demon now called the land its home.

In further efforts to uncover the cause further, Bob also hired professionals who scanned the property with ground penetrating radar in an effort to ensure that no bodies were buried there. However, as the crew scanned the earth, they found the remains of four bodies in the front yard near the old oak tree that stood there. Not wanting to further disturb the dead, Bob opted to commemorate them instead by placing crosses into the ground, to hopefully lay their souls to rest.

Although the death and despair more than likely attracted a demon, it still didn't answer the question as to why it came inside the house. One theory was that a disgruntled worker back when the home was being built placed a curse on it. That would account for the hidden shrine underneath the stairs. However, this couldn't be confirmed.

Several months after the investigation and turning in the information to the church, Bob and Lesa finally received some much-needed good news; the church finally approved an exorcism on their home. In September of 2005, an exorcist arrived to begin his work.

All appeared to be quiet and, truthfully, things went on without a hitch. The following day, the feel of the home was different, but Bob still felt as if something was lurking within its walls.

Roughly three months passed by without incident.

Then one night, Bob was in the basement doing some work to the hot water heater. He was suddenly imbued with that age old feeling of being watched – something that he had hoped was a thing of the past. Glancing up, he spotted the figure of a woman who then quickly darted into another basement room. Rushing into the room the woman had gone into, he saw nothing. Rushing up the stairs, he ran into Lesa and quickly told her that he saw something down there – that they needed another mass as soon as possible.

Together, they once again called Father Mike, who agreed to assist them. The following evening as the priest is mid mass, all three of them began to hear scratching coming from inside the walls. During the consecration of the wine, three distinct knocks were heard coming from inside the wall, something that should've been an impossibility. The mass concluded, but the war had not yet been won. It took another two years of frequent blessings to finally rid the house of the demon that inhabited it.

With this somewhat anticlimactic ending, because of course, not every story is going to be over the top, there are still many details I'd like to share with you as well as pose several questions. The reason they believed that a disgruntled worker may have placed a curse on the home during its construction was that the worker was jealous of the wealth of the man who built it – a doctor and his beautiful wife. However, apparently this doctor was known for performing illegal abortions in the house, tying back into the demon Molich and his consort Sathi.

Bob Cranmer's book, *The Demon of Brownsville Road*, has faced its share of criticism. One of the most significant points of contention is the lack of external verification for some of the historical claims, including the alleged bodies in the front yard. While the existence of Dr. James Merton Mahan has been confirmed, there are no documented records of any illegal activities, such as abortions, taking place during that period—though such records would likely be scarce if they existed at all.

The Cranmers, following their experiences in the home, haven't been without tragedy. In March of 2015, their son David passed away unexpectedly, sending him and his wife into a deep depression. They ultimately divorced in 2018, ending their 37-year marriage. After a decade of the house being fully cleansed of evil, Bob opened it as a bed and breakfast in 2019. It is now known as the Brownsville Road House. I truly wish all those involved the very best. The entire situation seemed not only traumatic to have to endure, but the more recent tragedy as well is just terrible.

With that being said, the story is a well-documented and textbook demonic haunting, and a terrifying one at that. Sometimes when you walk into a new environment and you get a terrible feeling, no matter how good the deal, you have to trust your gut. Because it just might save you years of anguish and spiritual despair.

# CHAPTER 2
## DEBORAH MOFFITT

How far would you go to save someone you loved? Would you spend all of your money trying to find the best treatment? Would you sacrifice a part of your very soul? When a caretaker performed what was supposed to be an ancient healing ritual on her friend's ailing grandmother, she unknowingly unleashed a terrifying and powerful demon – an entity that claimed to be one of the seven princes of hell. Will all those involved have their lives be torn apart as the malevolent demon haunts and torments their every waking moment? Or can they somehow be saved?

This is the story of the Deborah Moffitt case, also known as the Deadly Haunting or the Mr. Entity case. This absolutely terrifying story took place in California, and it perhaps is not one you should read alone or in the dark.

I sourced most of this from Deborah Moffitt's own words as well as several outside resources to try and form the most cohesive timeline possible. Not all names were able to be found but I've done my best to provide the most accurate story I can.

---

The story begins in 1984, when the grandmother-in-law of another woman who will become integral to our story, a woman named Deborah Moffitt, suffered a terrible and debilitating stroke. As a result of this unfortunate occurrence, she required around-the-clock care. To pay for her treatment and overall care, the family all chipped in and pooled together enough money to go ahead and hire a caretaker for her. They wanted someone who they could trust. After sifting through several candidates, they settled on a nearby neighbor and friend of the family – a middle-aged lady from Guatemala named Jaunita. The arrangement was both a godsend for Juanita and the family. It allowed Juanita to stay in the United States on her work visa and earn a nice living while providing aid to her friends, and it allowed the family's dear loved one to be taken care of by someone trusted and someone who genuinely cared.

Although this may seem somewhat controversial to some, this woman was an avid practitioner of Santeria. Santeria is an African diasporic religion that developed in Cuba during the late 19th century. It arose through a process of syncretism between the traditional Yoruba religion of West Africa, the Catholic form of Christianity, and Spiritism. Offerings to the oricha or various gods often include fruit, liquor, flowers and sacrificed animals.

In the months to come, Grandma's recovery was not going well. If anything, unfortunately, she was getting worse – much worse. Each day her state seemed to deteriorate more. Juanita worried about her friends, their grandmother, and her own wellbeing – thinking that perhaps if their grandma passed away that she would no longer be able to reside in California due to the loss of her job. This alongside the high cost of living and having to compete in the job market to keep her work visa valid, Juanita decided to take matters into her own hands. She decided to try an ancient Santeria healing spell in hopes that it would allow everyone involved but especially for grandma to do better. However, this ritual would prove to be anything but helpful.

Grandma did not get better; in fact, weeks following the ritual, she unfortunately passed away. Not only did she pass away and her family was devastated, but Jaunita indeed lost her job as a result of the woman's passing, simply because the caretaker position was no longer needed. I tried digging to uncover any and all details as to what happened to Juanita, but I was unable to find anything. My best guess is that perhaps with the loss of her caretaker position, she either couldn't afford to live in the area anymore and/or she went back to her native country. But those are just speculations on my part.

Deborah and her husband Bill inherited the home. In due time, they moved in following grandma's funeral. At first, all was rather normal and quiet within the house. But that ultimately changed with the birth of Debbie and Bill's first child in 1987, their first son.

Bill was a big sports memorabilia collector and had a particular spare bedroom dedicated to his hobby. He was especially fond of bobble heads, particularly baseball bobbleheads. It's important to note that they kept this room locked at all times, and Deborah's husband was the only person who had a key to enter it. One seemingly normal day, Deborah, Bill and a friend who lived nearby were headed into the house to show the friend just how extensive the collection had become. My best guess is that this gentleman was also very much into sports as well.

As they opened the door and began to walk into the room, they were shocked by what they saw; all of the bobble-heads on the toys had been removed. Every single one – from the ones on shelves to walls and cabinets. Stranger further, all of them had been laid together in the center of the floor to form a triangle of sorts. Not only was Bill upset and shocked, but the group weren't sure what to make of the happening. They somehow thought that someone had managed to break into the room to play a prank on them. But as to why they would've played such a prank on them and who would've done it was uncertain at best. After all, Bill was the only one with a key. Following this happening, only more bizarre things began to manifest. But, as they typically do, these manifestations started small.

Grandma, when she was alive, had been a very religious lady and in the room that was hers she had kept a bedside table with several Christian icons. Those of which contained both Jesus and the Virgin Mary. In honor of her, they had kept that table and those icons in the same place that she had left them. One morning, as Deborah was cleaning house, she noticed that a pair of her husband's briefs were draped over the biggest statue of Jesus on that very same table. Not only did her husband not change in that room, but she knew how close Bill was to his grandmother and how he would never have done anything disrespectful towards her or her things. Thinking that somehow it must've been an accident, she moved them and would later inform Bill of what she had found.

Unnerved at the strangeness yet again, the couple was unsure of what they were dealing with. However, as brand-new parents at that time, they didn't make solving the mystery a priority. Shortly after this happened, as their son was roughly a month old, yet another weird event would take place.

The couple had been out at a relative's house for dinner that evening. As food was ate, laughs were had, and dusk turned into night, they said their goodbyes and began traversing the winding roads back home. Upon arrival, they placed their keys in their door and stepped inside their house to begin to wind down. They flicked on their living room light switch and, as the lights illuminated, they saw a bizarre, enigmatic symbol drawn on the wall. Describing it later, Deborah would refer to it as something she had never seen before, like a series of triangles with tails. Yet again, a triangle was involved.

As they surveyed the room, they noticed that the symbols weren't just on this wall, however; they were on all of the walls in what would turn out to be the entire house, each of them appearing to have been drawn in some kind of charcoal-like substance.

Bill and Debbie again weren't sure of what to make of this. So they went to the logical headspace that perhaps someone was either pranking them or was breaking into their house. Both of which were unnerving, and both of which didn't make any sense. The pranking because they didn't really have a relationship with anyone like that, let alone given access to their house to anyone else. With someone intruding into their home, all of their doors and windows were locked, and none of their belongings or valuables were missing. It took several hours, but they eventually settled and fell asleep that night, despite the confusion and fear that someone was truly messing with them.

Five days later, as Bill rearranged his sports room, Deborah had taken up the task of cleaning the living room. On one of their walls there was a long shelf filled with little keepsakes and knick-knacks. She had glanced at the shelf while sweeping the floor and then looked back once again. As she would later describe, it was as if in the blink of an eye every single item on that shelf was turned backwards.

Upon coming out of his sports room, Bill was told by Deborah what had just taken place. At the time he refused to believe it, saying that she couldn't have seen it right to begin with.

However, Debbie knew what she had seen and just how impossible it would've been for them to be facing back- wards, because she was the only one who ever touched them. Despite trying to approach the situations logically, the illogical happenings only continued.

One week later, the two arrived home to discover a lamp sitting in the middle of their living room. With nothing else in the home out of place and nothing being wrong with any of the doors or windows, Debbie began to think that perhaps something was taking place that they couldn't understand. Bill harbored a deep fear of the paranormal and, with these realizations, somewhat went into a state of denial. He utterly refused to believe that something even remotely close could be taking place, let alone to them.

The lamp was placed back on the shelf where it was supposed to be and, following this, the two headed into the kitchen as Bill continued to try to rationalize and come up with excuses as to what was happening to them. After having a brief discussion and without hearing so much as the smallest of sounds, the couple re-emerged into their living room after roughly two to three minutes and were shaken to their core.

Before their very eyes, they found all of their furniture rearranged and stacked, one piece on top of the other. It was as if the entire room had been shifted upside down, but all within mere minutes and essentially in dead silence. At that point, there was no way to deny that they indeed were dealing with something beyond their comprehension.

With this realization, the two had completely different thoughts about the matter Deborah was apprehensive yet fascinated as to what could be happening, and Bill was surprisingly done denying what was taking place and was ready to move immediately and leave everything behind.

Debbie ended up placing the furniture back to normal in the living room. Bill didn't even want to be in the house, so he stood outside. He then refused to have anything to do with the activity from that point onward, essentially heading back into denial. To Deborah, the feeling wasn't a malevolent one. She saw it as almost a game of sorts. Whether this would prove to be detrimental or not later, is up to you.

With these feelings, she began to try and communicate with the presence daily, asking it to move things around to prove that it was there. Incredibly, it – whatever *it* was – would oblige. This action began a cat and mouse game that went on for roughly a week or so, until one day it randomly ceased.

Eventually, due to Bill's lack of comfort, the couple purchased and moved into the house next door, keeping their old home as a rental property for several years. That decision resulted in an eventual revolving door of tenants, some of them staying a year or so, but most just staying several months and leaving without giving a reason. It's important to note here that Bill would actually mention that the property could possibly be haunted, but most people laughed at the idea. Perhaps it was the times or perhaps people back then weren't as open minded to the world of the paranormal.

After several years, Bill and Debbie and several other surviving family members decided that they would sell their current homes and rental properties to purchase one large home and share the space as one big family. Once this was tackled and after several days of moving their own belongings to the new home, on the final day at their old house, something peculiar happened.

Deborah and a relative were gathering the final boxes from a room at the back of the house when suddenly they heard what they described as an explosion come from the kitchen. Dropping the boxes and bolting to the origin of the noise to see just what had happened, the two ladies were left speechless. All of the cabinets, the countertops, everything had been ripped from the walls, pieces of them lying all over the floor.

Before they could begin to process what had just taken place, they heard another loud explosion. This time it came from the bedroom they had just ran from. Running back, they again were astonished; every window in that back bedroom had been blown out with absolutely no explanation. Shards of glass littered the carpet and covered the final boxes they sought to move out.

Wasting no time, Debbie grabbed the relative by the arm and the two fled to the car, leaving the final boxes behind. They left the property as quickly as they could. It was within these moments that Deborah knew that whatever force they had been dealing with was not benevolent and, in fact, seemed to be hostile. Trying to come to terms with what had just happened, shaking with fear, she drove to the new house and the two spent the rest of the day trying to forget what had just happened.

For the first several days everything seemed to be quiet and calm as the family unpacked and got settled into their new life together. The new dynamic consisted of Deborah and Bill in the master bedroom downstairs and Bill's mother and father upstairs in the master bedroom. Two other relatives lived there as well, but I wasn't able to find additional details as to their exact relation or the time frame in which they ended up staying or leaving. But sometimes it's people that are haunted, not places.

Yet again, the Moffitts found themselves plagued by the same malevolent force that had previously stalked them from the shadows. The entity, like a feral beast who had simply been wounded, had nursed those wounds and seemed hellbent on revenge.

With the reappearance of this malevolent force certain members of the family were opposed to seeking assistance, while others felt that it was the necessary thing to do. Those opposing believed that they would be made a mockery of, considered crazy, and dismissed, leaving their reputations in shambles. But together they all believed that this problem was way too far out of their scope of normalcy to be able to tackle by themselves.

As the family stood divided against one another, the entity began to further isolate them individually. Not only could they certainly not have any guests over for fear that they too would be affected, but wherever they seemed to go, it would follow. It continuously made them so uncomfortable that they soon quit going places altogether for the most part.

For example, on one occasion, Deborah and Bill had been to one of Bill's friend's homes for dinner. They had a nice time, but this would be all too short lived. Upon their return to the house, on the kitchen table was the man's wallet. They had just been at his residence. As one might imagine, this was more than enough to chill someone to the bone. It was as if the entity was telling them to stop, or else someone else might get hurt. The Moffitts, now beside themselves with fear, were also worried just how they would explain to their friend how and why they had his wallet. Just what would he say or think?

In an effort try and seek some sort of help, Deborah was able to convince most of her family to go and visit a local but well-known psychologist to make sure it wasn't some kind of hysteria or that someone, herself included, hadn't somehow convinced themselves and everyone else that something paranormal was taking place when it wasn't.

The psychologist whose name was never disclosed was based out of Rancho Cucamonga, California and was apprehensive at first, and who can blame them. But after much explaining and meeting with the members of the family together and separately, the psychologist believed something strange was indeed taking place – something that they couldn't explain. They ultimately concluded naturally that they wouldn't be able to assist the family further. They told them that they needed to seek a para-psychologist, a religious institution, or some other party that studied those kinds of things.

Following the psychologist's advice, with most of Bill's family being religious – Catholic specifically – they sought the help of the church they attended. The church agreed to help them and sent a priest to bless their home. Several weeks later after their meeting, an older priest arrived at the house. Upon crossing the threshold of the home and into the foyer, the priest took out his holy water and began to sprinkle it on the walls around him, making the sign of the cross towards the hallway.

Oddly though, he refused to go any further into the home.

When asked, "Aren't you supposed to bless every room?" the priest would rebuttal, "No, no... this should be more than enough. I have to go now."

In further effort to get him to do what he was supposed to do, the family explained what had been taking place.

The priest made eye contact with Deborah and said, "Women when they get older, they tend to get a little crazy. Now excuse me I have to go."

Then without another word, he exited the door and left in his vehicle.

The family noticed he had seemed unnerved or slightly scared while he was at the house, but they were also totally flabbergasted at his odd response to them and their legitimate attempts to seek assistance. Thus, they were again left without any real help, believing the blessing to be rather subpar. Bill's mother, Lee, who was the most religious out of them all was simply crushed at the church's response and never truly seemed the same following the incident.

The entity seemed to latch onto this and began to feed upon her negativity following what had taken place. It began to torment her day in and day out. Some examples of what it would do to her would be to destroy her belongings, make her shoes disappear (one shoe would go missing from a pair), it destroyed her purse, wallet, credit cards and licenses multiple times. It hid things from her if it didn't destroy them.

It was as if it wanted to say, "I'm the one that's in control and you'll own things only if I say that you can."

Having very bad eyesight most of her life, the creature would take her glasses away or smash them. While she was unable to see, it manifested itself as a large, terrifying, foreboding figure which to Lee seemed like a massive black mist, often touching or abusing her.

The demon also began to have a peculiar obsession with knives. Knives began appearing stuck in walls and, frighteningly, under chairs so if someone sat down, they would greatly injure themselves. Stranger still, these knives were not the family's knives – they had absolutely no idea where they came from. The intensity of the knife situation escalated to the point that they were being placed upright under pillows, and Lee again seemed to bear the brunt of the abuse.

The Moffitts were seemingly beat down into a corner, and as they sat there, they collectively wondered just how they could defend themselves against something they couldn't see. Just how could they defeat an entity that shouldn't even exist?

The torture continued for the family as a whole, but it was being done as if the demon was wanting to communicate some kind of a message. One day, an unmistakable sign appeared, indeed communicating a message. In what would be the first of many, the entity began to write on various mirrors in soap.

The first message appeared to Lee, saying:

*Talk to me.*

This particular message appeared shortly after the family had come home from getting groceries, trying to gain some sense of normalcy. At first, wanting to make sure it wasn't one of the family members playing a trick on the others – which would be pretty horrible at this point to be honest – they cleaned the mirror thoroughly. Everyone then convened in the bedroom together, saying that if there was additional writing on the mirror following them cleaning it in the next several minutes, then the event is indeed real.

After approximately fifteen minutes of waiting, they reluctantly re-entered the bathroom to find this written on the mirror:

*Nini .. don't go into the attic.*

Upon reading this, Lee froze in her tracks. There was only one person who ever called her that nickname or was even aware of it, and that was her long-deceased sister.

From here, the days turned into nights and the messages continued, becoming more sadistic, controlling and abusive. For the next year, the family was held hostage by what they now believed to be a demonic entity. The messages were more or less commands or insults, and the spirit would not answer any of their questions in response to them. It got to the point that when and if they sought to go places for any reason, they had to ask permission. Otherwise, they would have car issues or damage, such as broken windshields, headlights, or even engine failure.

Eventually, out of frustration, Bill's father would ask the name of the entity in hopes that they could figure out just what it wanted and why it tormented them all in an effort to put a stop to it. Upon asking, they would finally receive an answer. There, scribbled on the mirror, was the name Prince.

Following them receiving this name, they heard a commotion coming from all over the house below them. Rushing down the stairs, they found many of their items and furniture broken into pieces and several symbols scribbled on the walls and floors. The symbol, as vaguely mentioned before, involved triangles and small offshoot characters. This shape over time would be scribbled, carved, and even burned into walls, floors and furniture within the home.

Following this event, each day seemed to mirror the last. It almost always started with the family having to put the home back together. Everything would be in complete disarray upon them waking up each and every morning.

Wherever they went, *it* went. If they went out to eat, even upon asking permission, when they would return the name tag of the waiter or waitress would be on the table. One time, a massive bite was taken out of the mother-in-law's steak just mere seconds after she received it with no rational origin as to how it happened.

This state of utter imprisonment and constant battle with an enemy they couldn't see led the family to seek additional help to try and free themselves of the hell they now lived in. They went through a long list of reputable people and organizations to try and escape, but nothing seemed to work. This included Loyd Auerbach and his connections to various paranormal societies. One such society consisted of Christopher Chacon, another well-known name in the paranormal world, and his investigation team. They were unable to make sense of the situation and ultimately couldn't help the Moffitts.

The Moffitts reached out to various religious organizations of differing faiths; they tried having magicians come out, and they even contacted Thelma Moss, who would send Kerry Gaynor out to investigate. This was the very same Thelma Moss and Kerry Gaynor of the San Pedro Haunting and Doris Bither case. Yet no one could get rid of it. No number of blessings, rituals or investigations seemed to work. They had shamans out, wiccans, and even the Warrens, and still, no one could help them.

As the years trickled by ever slowly, agonizingly, things had not improved. Rather it had become so violent and dangerous within the house that the entire family – both Bill's parents, Bill, Deborah, and their son – were all sleeping in the living room together and would not separate for fear of what would happen. The demon known as Prince had taken over the entire upstairs.

One night, Deborah, on behalf of her mother-in-law decided to risk it and head upstairs to grab some medication that had been left behind that she desperately needed. Upon opening the door and walking into this now claimed domain, every fiber of her being was telling her to turn around and run. Persisting, she made her way past all the broken furniture and utter chaos to where the medication was. After grasping the bottle in her palm and turning around to head back towards the stairs, she heard a low, growling noise behind her originating from the attic.

There in the flesh was the disembodied head of a grotesque creature, grayish in appearance with the blackest, most soulless eyes imaginable. A twisted horn emerged from its temple and up over its head. This caused an involuntarily scream to erupt from Deborah's mouth, straight from the depths of her soul. She then, with everything she had, ran back downstairs. She believed that this indeed was the entity known as Prince's true form.

Things from here continued to go downhill and, as they do, escalated in intensity and torture. One morning, Lee went to grab something from the pantry in the kitchen, a place they felt safe in for the most, since it was on the ground level of the house. As she opened the door and stepped into the walk-in pantry to grab the item she was after, suddenly the door behind her slammed shut.

She then felt invisible hands grab her throat and squeeze – picking her up, her feet leaving the floor and dangling. As she struggled to breathe. feeling as if it was the end, when everything began to go black, the hands suddenly released and she collapsed down to the floor.

Her husband was first to rush to her aid. She was hysterical after coming back to consciousness. Prince clearly had the power to take a human life, or so it seemed, but chose not to. Was this because it wanted to feed upon misery versus taking a soul, or for some other reason? Did demons perhaps have rules they had to abide by?

Deborah had finally reached her breaking point. She stormed into the upstairs bathroom and demanded answers from Prince. She told the being that the family was no longer to be touched, that they would respect its space, but it had to respect theirs.

Surprisingly, Deborah began to receive replies on the mirror in the same fashion as the entity had always communicated, by writing on it. Prince said he would no longer bother any other member of the family, but that Lee had been promised to him many moons ago and that he had come to collect.

Deborah asked the creature to elaborate, and for the next hour the entity wrote on the mirror. Deborah would erase the writing, wait, go back, read and repeat, until the full story had been told. Not wanting to allow Prince to have any sort of power over her, Deborah decided to start referring to him as Mr. Entity, essentially leaving him a nameless face but with a respectable title as they agreed upon.

Here I wanted to mention a few of the smaller details I uncovered, from the time of grandma's old house till now. The family did also experience paranormal manifestations we commonly come across, such as putrid odors, knocking, and banging throughout the home with no rational origin, and rarely seen but somewhat indicative of a more powerful entity. They also experienced infestation. Some people experience insects from what I've come across. The Moffitts had a terrible rat problem, but one that came out of nowhere and then disappeared roughly two weeks later, again with no cause.

Another disturbing thing that Mr. Entity had taken to was ending the lives of the family's dogs if it didn't get what it wanted. There are more details on what happened to several of the pets, but the details are gruesome and it's really not necessary to include this info. Just that it happened, and it happened more than once in this case.

Often times the ending to these kinds of cases can be anti-climactic and this one, despite how incredible of a story it is, is no exception. After six agonizing years with dozens of seasoned paranormal investigators, religious leaders, shamans, occult magicians, and more assisting the Moffitts with the demon known as Prince, no relief was provided for all of those years. Prince continued to plague their lives until one day, the entity simply was no longer there.

Following this creature's departure, Debbie, Bill, and the family would destroy lots of the photos, but keep some in storage in the attic. They also stopped speaking about what they had endured for years, for fear that whatever it was would come back.

Thankfully, for whatever reason, it never did – or hasn't, yet.

Debbie and Bill went on to raise their family and eventually moved on. Debbie became an author and spiritual advisor, not only to assist others who may have experienced something similar, but to also share her extensive knowledge and hellish waking life that she and her family endured under the reign of Prince. I highly recommend checking out her books.

As we conclude our story, as always, I'd like to give some of the thoughts I've had while researching this very unhinged and perplexing case.

Was this spirit demonic? A familiar of some sort? A Djinn, as we'll see in a minute, or perhaps something pretending to be more than it was?

We will never have definitive answers to these questions, but in my opinion Prince or Mr. Entity – whatever it was – was certainly incredibly powerful. Especially given the destruction it was alleged to have perpetrated given the descriptions given by Debbie in various interviews, her own books, and photos provided for both by her.

Again, in my opinion, the entity was certainly demonic. I think true demonic hauntings are not only extremely rare but incredibly dangerous, with the spirits having the ability to cause tangible physical and mental harm to all those involved. Demons aren't all powerful, but they are more intelligent than we are and can foresee things that we simply cannot.

When explaining the story as to why it sought and or tormented Lee so hard, that apparently, she had been promised to it many moons or years ago, this is what leads me to believe that perhaps someone in their lineage promised their descendants in exchange for something. Whether it was money, fame, what have you, I'm not sure, but perhaps the entity had finally come to claim its debt – the soul that was bartered during said exchange.

Now I don't think that it was a human spirit pretending to be something it wasn't. A prince of hell, I'm not totally convinced of, but in most hauntings the beings don't have half the ability to do what Prince supposedly did. Many years following the events of the Moffitt family haunting, during an interview with the great late Art Bell, Debbie spoke with a guest who seemingly identified the symbol that Prince or Mr. Entity had supposedly used. It was a symbol he had come across during his time in the army while in Afghanistan. Further investigation revealed on his behalf that the symbol was that of Iblis (eeblis), which is known as a Djinn from the Quran. It's known as the leader of the devils in Islam. Iblis was thrown out of heaven after he refused to prostrate himself before Adam. It's also known as the father of bitterness. This certainly would explain the power behind Prince, that's for sure.

All around, this case is incredible, perplexing, and terrifying, when taking things at Deborah Moffitts word. I can only vaguely relate to just how terrible her and her family's experience dealing with this thing must've been, and one thing is for certain. Whether Prince was indeed a prince of hell as it claimed to be or just a very powerful entity, it certainly tormented this family as if they had been sent to the seventh circle themselves.

# CHAPTER 3
## BOBBY MACKEY'S

When a man goes to fulfill his dream, what price is he willing to pay?

Is it worth losing everything he loves? Is it worth awakening an old evil?

This story is a strange and unique tale of a place where a portal to hell is said to exist, with a force that seems determined to attack the living and overtake the weak.

Welcome to the untold story of the Demonic Bobby Mackey's Music World.

---

Our story begins in Wilder, Kentucky where an abandoned music hall sits off the banks of the Licking River. Country singer Bobby Mackey visits the property with a real estate agent, in search of fulfilling a lifelong dream. After hitting success in the music scene, allowing him to leave his job at the railroad and pursue music full time, he's been on the road touring for nearly 12 years.

He loves what he does, but he loves someone more – his wife, Janet, who is pregnant with their first child. They want to settle down, plant some roots, and start a family. He thinks this could be the perfect opportunity.

Bobby has always wanted to open a music hall, a nightclub suited for his particular style of country. Wandering the ballroom and gazing at the now empty bar of this former rock and roll venue, he can visualize exactly what he's been dreaming about for all these years. And so, after the tour, with a few moments of thought, he decides to purchase it.

Little did he know he was purchasing so much more than he bargained for.

Later that day, Bobby would return with Janet to show her the place that they were now in the process of purchasing. From the moment she laid eyes on the property, Janet felt that there was something ominous about it. The energy about the place just felt off.

After unlocking the front door and stepping inside for the first time, she surveys the inside with Bobby. At his recommendation, she went into the kitchen alone while he grabbed some items from their truck. As she walked around, looking at the various equipment, she began to hear a muffled voice calling out.

From the sink.

A gargled, female voice rang out, but no matter how hard she tried, she couldn't make out what it was trying to say. As she experienced this, it deeply disturbed her.

Calling out for Bobby, she heard nothing in response. She then ran out the kitchen doors and into the ballroom where she could see Bobby starting to walk back in through the main door of the establishment. She asked who he was talking to, and he told her no one, that it was just him and her in the entire building.

She told him she heard voices, but Bobby dismissed her. He thought that perhaps hormones were affecting her on account of the pregnancy. She repeated that she didn't have a good feeling about the building, and time would tell that she would be right.

Although his wife disapproved and wanted the two of them to sleep on the idea some more, Bobby was transfixed by the vision he had for a literal dream come true scenario. In his own words, "I couldn't be stopped. I had to have the place."

Shortly after this conversation took place, he signed the paperwork, attained the banknote, and officially owned the property. After signing his name on the dotted line, Bobby would never be able to look back.

Although Janice didn't want him to, she still tried to be a supportive wife – despite the growing fear that gripped her in the establishment. She still assisted Bobby with mild renovations, to the best of her ability.

One day as Bobby painted some walls and Janice swept around the bar, a stranger walked through the front doors of the music hall. Introducing himself as Carl Lawson, he told Bobby that he had worked for the previous owners as a handyman. Unfortunately, he had been out of a job ever since the club had closed due to several particularly brutal murders taking place upon its grounds. The club's final year was the most brutal, with six homicides taking place.

In later interviews he would say, "Any bar or nightclub is going to have its fair share of fights. But the amount of violence that seemed to take place here – the type of crowd it attracted – seemed abnormal to me."

Upon hearing Carl's story, Bobby quickly dismissed the idea of the nightclub becoming a hotspot for violence. He believed that the type of music was what could've caused people to be more violent. Since the club was going to play traditional country music instead of rock, he believed it would attract a very different crowd.

After a brief inquiry about his skillset, Bobby decides to hire Carl as a full-time caretaker and handyman for the nightclub. In due time, as per their arrangement, he would live in the attic of the property. As the renovations ramped up to get the club ready for opening, Carl and Janice found themselves working on projects together throughout the building. They began to get along and their friendship was like a big sister and little brother.

One afternoon, Janice asked Carl if he had ever experienced anything strange inside the club. To her surprise, he told her that he believed that there was much more than met the eye with the place – that there was some kind of force that made people violent there. He added that the two should keep a lookout for one another.

Following this brief conversation, Carl would go back to painting walls near the stage and Janice would resume washing dishes in the kitchen. As she toiled away, she began to hear an all too familiar sound – a muffled, gurgling kind of sound, similar to what she had heard the very first time she had visited the property. To her absolute horror, she glanced down into the sink that the sound was emanating from and saw a thick, blood-like liquid oozing up from the drain. It then began to fill up the sink.

As she stepped backwards, preparing to call for Carl's help, she felt someone – or some*thing* – grab the back of her head and physically push her towards the sink. For what seemed like an eternity, she braced herself with her hands against the sink as she screamed for help, only to feel the pressure release as soon as Carl ran into the kitchen. As she fell backwards, she began to hysterically tell Carl about what had just happened, that something tried to hurt her and the sink was full of blood.

However, upon examining the sink, Carl didn't see anything. Neither did Janet; it was completely clean.

The two continued to talk until Janet calmed down. They concluded that whatever presence dwelled within the walls of this club was not friendly, and it was not playing games. It had become violent.

Once she collected herself, Janet tracked Bobby down and confronted him about what had just happened to her. He didn't believe her.

Thinking his wife had gone crazy, he called Carl over and told him that he didn't want him filling her head with any more ideas about ghosts.

Janet retorted that she had in fact asked Carl if he had experienced anything, not the other way around. Nonetheless, Bobby refused to believe either of them. He didn't believe in ghosts or the paranormal, and his only concern was getting the bar up and running so that he could make his money back. In due time, he would see that perhaps they were right.

Within a week of those conversations taking place, another event took place. A police officer by the name of Larry Hornsbee made his usual patrol rounds which happened to go by the club. As he drove through the parking lot, he spotted a figure behind the window and the door of the club open. Thinking that someone had broken in, he quickly called it in and asked for backup to investigate.

Once another officer arrived, the pair cautiously made their way inside with guns drawn and flashlights out. As they scanned the bar for the potential burglar, they found nothing. They didn't hear anything, either. It was eerily quiet.

That was until music began blasting from behind the stage. Jazz played and the sounds of people laughing and talking could be heard. As they announced their presence, the officers made their way to where the music was coming from.

As soon as Officer Hornsbee threw back the curtain, the music stopped.

Unsure of what to make of the situation, the two officers looked at each other and became even more unnerved when the front door slammed shut. They raced through the club and out the front door, ready to pursue whoever they believed to be there.

After a thorough search, they again found no one. It's also important to note that there was little to no wind that night.

Hornsbee would later say, "The two of us were stunned, but I couldn't put in a report that we encountered some kind of ghost. I would be the laughing stalk, or they'd send me to a psychiatrist. So, I simply put that we had gone through the building but did not find any burglars. But I know what I heard and what I saw, and I wasn't the only one there."

Just two nights later, Officer Hornsbee found himself outside of the nightclub again, but this time for a very different reason. A woman had lost control of her vehicle and hit the light pole in the nightclub's parking lot – a fatal crash.

Not having anything to cover the body once it was removed from the vehicle, as the officer called it in a woman tapped him on the shoulder and handed him a tablecloth. She then walked back into the nightclub. Once the scene was clear, accompanied by several officers, Hornsbee knocked on the door in hopes of thanking the woman for her assistance. However, the doors were locked and there were no signs of life within the club.

The following morning, the officer and his partner contacted Bobby Mackey at the club to inform him of what had taken place. They told him of the woman who came out of his club, brought them a tablecloth, and then went back inside – thinking she was a waitress.

Bobby shocked them by telling them that he hadn't hired any staff yet besides Carl. The club would've been completely locked up, and he and his wife were sound asleep when the event would've occurred. Not sure of what to make of this, the officers simply thanked him and left. Bobby – despite the credibility of the officers – still didn't believe that there was anything supernatural about his nightclub.

Later that afternoon, as Carl was changing lightbulbs upstairs, he accidentally dropped and broke the last good one he had. As he walked down the stairs to grab several more, he encountered Janet. She inquired about the sound. After he explained, she sent him off while she decided to sweep up the glass at the top of the stairs. As she finished sweeping the glass into a pile and turned to grab the dustpan, she was shoved from behind.

Panicked, she began to hyperventilate because it was dangerously close to the edge of the stairs. Suddenly, she was pushed again – causing her to fall down the stairs.

She was found by Carl who screamed for Bobby. Before he got to them, she told Carl that something pushed her down those stairs. The three then loaded up as quickly as possible and rushed to the hospital.

The fall caused Janet to go into premature labor and give birth to a baby girl weighing only one pound and fifteen ounces. The next several weeks were tense as the new parents monitored their baby, unsure if she was going to make it. Thankfully, against the odds, she did.

Approximately three weeks later, as his newly born daughter and wife were released from the hospital, Bobby prepared for the grand opening of what he aptly named Bobby Mackey's Music World. Although he was present physically, he was numb emotionally. He felt as if the world was on his shoulders. That night could make or break the club's reputation and, coming off the heels of what had just taken place within his family, he was raw to say the least.

He overheard a customer talking about ghosts and that almost sent him over the edge. He found Carl behind the bar and confronted him. He told him that he would no longer have a job if he continued to tell customers about ghosts. He didn't want to hear any more about it because he had to focus on the business for his family. He didn't want to hear any more about this nonsense, and that the hall would be known for great country music – not for ghosts that didn't exist.

Although he felt a presence and he and Janet had spoken several times about their experiences, Carl was between a rock and a hard place. He decided to hold his tongue and agree with the man who was paying his salary.

Several weeks after the grand opening, Carl moved into the attic above the club which had since been converted into an apartment of sorts – another perk of being the handyman at Bobby Mackey's music world.

But as a result of moving forward, he had to spend every night there. Alone.

He felt as if he wasn't just a handyman, but a caretaker of sorts. As if something kept drawing him back to the property. Unless he had a pressing matter to leave, he wouldn't. He would just stay there, protecting the club and watching over it.

One night, he finished stacking the chairs on top of the tables around the bar. As he stepped towards the light switch to turn them out and head to his loft, he heard a strange noise behind him. Turning to observe where the source could be coming from, he saw the chairs begin to rattle and shake. As he stared in disbelief, the chairs were flung in all different directions. This terrified Carl and he rushed up to his apartment, where he barricaded himself in for the night.

Over the next several weeks, he was in a state of denial about what he had seen. Trying to come to terms with his trauma, Carl took to cleaning. One night he found himself down in the storage room of the club, where he found a loose board on the floor. Upon prying it out to then replace it, he found a bundle of old looking cloth.

He picked it up and unraveled it in his hands. Inside the cloth was an old journal. As he read it, he discovered that it had belonged to a woman named Johanna, who had been a dancer at the club during the 1930s. Over the next several days, he read through the entire journal and learned her story.

She had fallen in love with a musician who her father despised. Her father had told her that he would kill this man before he'd let him marry her. One day, the man she loved suddenly wasn't around the club – he had gone missing, and she had just found out that she was pregnant. Thinking her father had something to do with it, she calculated, planned, and then poisoned her father.

And then herself.

The final entry in the diary proclaimed that she would roam the halls of the club for all eternity, waiting for her lover to return to her.

After finishing her journal while lying in his bed, Carl decided to finally get some sleep. However, a storm was brewing outside – and also inside of the club.

He woke up choking and coughing, unable to catch his breath. Lightning illuminated the room and thunder rocked the club. With rain smacking the windows behind his head, Carl finally managed to catch his breath. However, he was unable to go back to sleep.

Several minutes later, the power went out.

Being the handyman that he was, he grabbed a flashlight and made his way towards the basement, where the breaker box was located. He tried to flip the breaker back, but he was unsuccessful and dropped his flashlight, which then rolled towards the center of the basement room.

Not ever having spent much time down there, Carl stumbled upon a latch which he had never seen before as he picked up his flashlight. As any curious mind would, he decided to open it up. With only the lightning lighting up the room on occasion, along with his flashlight, he discovered what appeared to be a well in the basement of Bobby Mackey's.

Not sure of what to make of it, he closed the latch back up and began to make his way towards the breaker box once again. Just several feet into making his way back, he froze in his tracks.

Standing before him were the apparitions of two men. Although he could barely make out their faces, what he could see when the lightning struck looked menacing. He stepped back into the basement room as he began to hyperventilate from fear.

Carl heard footsteps coming towards him, and then sounds of a woman screaming coming from underneath his feet. He was standing directly over the well.

He then felt a presence overtake him as he lost consciousness.

Upon daybreak, he opened his eyes and rushed back up the stairs. Returning several minutes later with a blessed vial of holy water that he had in his possession, he believed that if he poured the holy water down the well it would help keep whatever evil that was down there from coming back up. He did just that and then returned back upstairs to begin the workday with Bobby. However, his actions didn't seem to work.

Over the course of the next 3 weeks, Carl seemed to undergo a radical change in personality. He seemed darker, angrier and more aggressive, which was a far cry from the timid and easy-going guy that Bobby and Janet had come to know. His moods became unpredictable.

Bobby would later say, "It got to the point that I wasn't sure which Carl I was talking to on a daily basis."

Carl began to carry a crucifix with him, in hopes of warding off the evil he now believed was coming from the well in the basement and attempting to take over his body.

These strange interactions between Bobby, Carl and Janet prompted multiple arguments between Bobby and Janet. Janet believed that something spiritual was affecting Carl, and Bobby believed that the two of them were nuts. He had more important things, like the business to worry about.

Several weeks later, in an attempt to further expand his business's reach, Bobby filmed a commercial for his establishment. He had his friend and journalist, Doug

Hensley, present to hopefully get a good article circulating before too long.

Upon speaking with Doug about how things were going once the commercial shoot had finished, Bobby confided in him that business wise things were going pretty well, but his wife and Carl Lawson couldn't stop talking about ghosts.

Although he didn't believe in it, Doug was intrigued. Being a writer, he asked why Bobby had kept this a secret. He responded that he didn't want the reputation of the music hall being tainted by ghosts because a lot of people were scared of ghosts. He also believed it would affect the type of people who would come. Doug asked if he could speak with Carl and Janet, and Bobby agreed.

The following afternoon, Doug interviewed Carl and Janet without Bobby present. He wanted to try and understand what they thought they were experiencing. Upon asking Carl his thoughts, Doug was met with a straightforward answer: Carl told him that the place was evil.

Over the course of the interview, the two told him their experiences. including Carl discovering Johanna's diary, the well in the basement and the two men he saw that stormy night. He said that he only continued to stay at the property as its caretaker to protect Janet and Bobby from whatever malevolent force infested its walls. He believed that the force, despite his best efforts to leave, always seemed to draw him back.

Being a skeptic, but accepting the stories at face value, Doug concluded the interview by thanking them. The following day he compiled his notes and went to the local library to research the history of the property. Believing that Carl Lawson was schizophrenic, he didn't think any of the information would check out. As he began to dig, his mind started to change.

Upon laying eyes on a 19th century article from the Kentucky post, he was strangely intrigued. In 1897, two men – one by the name of Alonzo Walling and the other by the name of Scott Jackson – were hung for the murder of a woman named Pearl Bryan. Bryan's headless corpse was found near the site of an old slaughterhouse in Wilder.

She had been a Sunday school teacher and was five and a half months pregnant at the time of her demise. Scott Jackson was a former boyfriend of Pearl's, and Alonzo Walling had been his roommate at dental school. It was alleged that the two attempted to remove the child but failed and removed Pearl's head in an attempt to keep her from being identified.

Rumors quickly circulated that the two were practicing Satanists and in a ritual sacrifice to Satan himself, killed Pearl and her unborn child. Despite several searches around Kentucky and in the Ohio river, her head was never found. The only thing the killers told the authorities was that it was in a deep, dark place and would never be seen again.

As the two men were asked to give their final words before meeting their own fates at the gallows, Alonzo Walling gave an eerie last couple sentences. He said that he would come back from hell and haunt everyone involved in his trial, as well as the location where Pearl Bryan's head was located.

When searching for Pearl's head, bloodhounds lead investigators to the old slaughterhouse and although it was never proven, it was speculated that the two men had disposed of it by dropping it in the old well located in the basement as part of their ritual. The club now known as Bobby Mackey's Music World rests on top of the foundation of that very same slaughterhouse.

Between the time it was a slaughterhouse and when it became a nightclub, there were documented incidents involving law enforcement catching various groups and cults performing rituals in the basement around that well. They typically performed blood sacrifices of small animals as offerings, believing it to be a portal of sorts, due to how much blood had been spilt and soaked into the land. When the property had been a slaughterhouse, a main drainpipe guided the blood from the floor to where it would then drain off into the Licking River.

Doug began to speculate that the two men Carl had seen that night when he discovered the well could've very well have been the spirits of Alonzo Walling and Scott Jackson. Because he believed that the two had for whatever reason, satanic or not, had disposed of her head in that well and now haunted the grounds of the club.

The mystery also deepens – through his research, Doug Hensley went from hard skeptic to a convinced believer. He came to believe angry spirits inhabited the grounds of Bobby Mackey's Music World and through his research he also noticed a disturbing pattern. Pearl Bryan had been five and a half months pregnant at the time of her demise. According to her diary entries, Johanna was five and a half months pregnant right before her demise. Janet had also been five and a half months pregnant, when she was pushed down the stairs.

Once he had finished researching and putting the story together with that research, he asked to meet with Bobby, Janet, and Carl. Several weeks later, he told them about his convictions as well as the pattern. The pattern in particular, given what Janet had experienced, concerned him the most. It prompted him to ask Bobby to allow them to do something about it.

Although he didn't personally believe in spirits, Bobby had known Doug a long time and knew that he was a sensible person with a good head on his shoulders. So, going against his wishes, Bobby gives him the go ahead to do what he thinks needs to be done. It took several more weeks, but arrangements were made.

In an effort to bring peace to whatever spirits seemed to be lurking within the nightclub, a psychic by the name of Patricia Michelle was brought in. She was given no prior knowledge of the history or story behind it. Upon her arrival, she met Carl Lawson and he quickly began to say what he thought was within the club. She asked him to please keep any information to himself, so she wouldn't be influenced by it as she did her walk-through.

During her time roaming Bobby Mackey's, Patricia sensed and spoke with a spirit. Upon asking her name, she was told it was Johanna. When asking Johanna why she remained here, she was told that she knew that she was dead but that she had chosen to stay.

In regards to what she believed to be taking place there, Patricia Michelle would later say, "I believe that there are spirits inhabiting Bobby Mackey's establishment and I believe that they have chosen to stay there rather than move on and face what they believe will be a place where they burn for all eternity."

Upon surveying the basement, she asked to open up the latched board on the floor to reveal the well below. As she stared down into the well, she gasped and told everyone present that there was the head of a woman there. She then fell back and was overcome with a horrible bout of nausea. It was coupled by cold sweats and the spins until she left the club.

Several hours later, she returned once she was feeling able bodied again, to meet with everyone and discuss how she felt about what she had seen and uncovered. As she sat down at a table with Janet, Doug, Carl, and several of her own people, she noticed that Carl was trembling and hyperventilating. She then saw two men standing behind him and the feeling she got when she saw them was one of overwhelming dread and malice.

She believed that these spirits had been oppressing Carl and were trying to wear him down to the point to where they could use his body. Fearing that Carl would soon become possessed, Patricia recommended that he seek the help of a minister to help break this attachment. After divulging the rest of her feelings to everyone, Patricia left.

Several days later, Doug contacted and brought in a Pentecostal minister to meet with Carl. Upon stepping foot in the club, the minister told Doug before meeting Carl this was the evilest place he had ever stepped foot in. He had been doing this for years and never saw or felt anything like it. He said if Carl was experiencing what he said he was experiencing, let alone living in a place like this, that he certainly was or was on the cusp of being demonically possessed and needed help immediately.

Upon meeting Carl for the first time, he knew what he had said to be true. He followed Carl into the kitchen where the two sat at a table together. For his own documentation, he placed a video camera to record their interaction, and the minister began to pray over him.

As he prayed aloud, Carl began to contort and grimace. When asked his name, he spoke back to the preacher in a voice that was not his own. He responded with, "My name is Alonzo, and I pray to no God."

The minister then commanded Alonzo to leave Carl's body. Carl then fell back off of his chair and onto the floor and began to contort and scream. The minister called for the other men to come and surround Carl. Due to the violent outbursts, he didn't want to be injured, nor did he want Carl to injure himself. As the men restrained Carl, he began to scream at them in Latin, which the minister spoke.

However, he went from Latin to speaking English backwards, saying, "Natas ma I. Natas ma I." Or forwards, I am Satan, which they wouldn't know until they watched the tape back later.

After an hour of praying, and demanding that the spirit leave Carl's body, Carl screamed in what sounded like two men screaming in unison for several seconds. Everyone there felt a cold rush of wind blow past them as Carl lay silent, breathing heavily. He finally came to several minutes later and didn't recall anything that took place.

He would later say, "When I woke up everyone was looking at me and I was on the floor, and I didn't know what had happened."

Several days following the exorcism, Carl decided that it was time for him to move on. He no longer felt tethered to the property and said that he began to feel like himself again. He thanked the Mackey's for employing and befriending him and then left in search of a new opportunity.

Following Carl's departure, Janet Mackey did not want to be at the club given everything she had experienced. After that, she instead opted to stay at home with their now healthy baby girl.

Before we get to the end of this perplexing paranormal story, I do have some additional history I'd like to share with you about Bobby Mackey's. We're familiar with Pearl Bryan and the fact that the property was built on the foundation of an old slaughterhouse. We know that between the time of its demolishing and rebuilding as a club, it was a supposed hotbed for satanic cult activity, and further investigation proved Johanna's existence as well. Once it was rebuilt and resold, the club has an interesting story.

It reopened as a roadhouse that became an illicit bar and gambling den, known better by the name The Primrose. It was a speakeasy run by the mob and as a result of its owners, it became a hotbed for violence.

It changed ownership in the 1950s and changed its name to The Latin Quarter. Johanna was a dancer there and the daughter of the club's owner. She had fallen in love with a singer named Robert Randall and ended up pregnant with his child. Having a strong dislike for Robert, her father found this out and was enraged. He did in fact have Robert killed as a result. Depressed by the death of Robert, Johanna then poisoned herself in the basement, right above where the well was.

Despite this research, her diary and the poisoning of her father could not be confirmed.

The Latin Quarter remained open until 1978, until a series of shootings and sub-sequential law enforcement pressure forced it to close its doors. It was then purchased by Bobby Mackey several months later. To this day, Bobby Mackey still says that he himself has never experienced any supernatural occurrences.

Many people who have visited, however, have. A sign now hangs within Bobby Mackey's walls that serves as a warning to all patrons, that the club cannot be held liable for anything that happens to them as a result of the ghosts. Despite still not being a believer, given everything he saw his mantra has long since been, 'Come for the ghosts and stay for the music.'

If it was haunted, could there have been a force perhaps keeping him blind to it all? Driving and keeping his hunger alive?

And if Bobby Mackey's music world is indeed haunted, perhaps underneath its floorboards, deep in the bowels of its basement, inside of the old well, a portal to hell still exists.

And whatever evil that lingers there perhaps slithers out of it whenever it feels the proper opportunity to exploit the weak.

Don't let it be you.

# CHAPTER 4
## SMURL HAUNTING

After a flood destroys their home, a family is forced to relocate to a new home which they believe is going to be a fresh new start. However, it turns out to be a fresh new hell instead. From demonic attacks, nightmarish visuals, and terrifying manifestations, this is one haunting story you won't want to miss.

This is the untold story of the Smurl Haunting in Pennsylvania and the monstrous creature that stalked its walls. The timeline of events is rough at best, but I have done my best to make the most coherent retelling of the story, so please keep that in mind.

***

It's 1973. Raging floods as a result of Hurricane Agnes have destroyed the homes of many families and one such family was the Smurls. The Smurl family consisted of

Janet and Jack Smurl, and their four young children, Heather, Shannon, Karen and Don. With their home destroyed in Wilkes-Barre, Pennsylvania, they felt as if they had been uprooted and tossed about like the rushing waters that took their house.

The Smurls decided to temporarily relocate to West Pittson, where Jack's parents lived. After explaining the situation and staying with the couple for a short time, they were surprised and ultimately blessed when Jack's parents proposed an idea to them. They had found an old duplex, a bit of a fixer upper also in West Pittson. The two of them could live on one side while Jack, Janet, and the kids lived on the other. That way they could look out for one another, and of course spend more time together.

Not in a position (or wanting) to say no, Jack and Janet humbly accepted their offer. All too soon, they would be confronted with the question: was this blessing truly a curse?

With Jack's parents covering the cost, they quickly found themselves settled into their new home, a recently purchased duplex. Located on Chase Street there in West Pittson, the home would need some work, but the neighborhood seemed friendly and inviting, a good place to raise a family.

The family collectively put their efforts into repainting, retooling, and other repairs. In no time, the slightly run down home was feeling fresh, vibrant, and modern, making the Smurls feel ever more at home and hopeful for the future. However, this would not last forever, for it seemed that each time they banged a hammer, each time they drove a nail into a wall, and with every drop of paint, they woke something up within the house itself. Something that perhaps had been slumbering there for quite some time.

During this time, small episodes of strangeness began to manifest. Seeming rather benign at first, tools began to disappear only to reappear hours later in different spots. Old stains that covered the walls began to seep through the fresh coats of paint that were meant to cover them, and several appliances in their kitchen had mysteriously caught fire, even though they were unplugged. Along with these oddities, the family also began to smell awful odors that overwhelmed the entire house, like an omnipresent floating cloud of rotting meat that hung over them, only to disperse mere moments after being detected. Despite these weird events, the family didn't really think much of it. They were just thankful to have a roof over their heads.

Jack and Janet continued to rebuild their lives. Fortunately, Jack had since gotten a better job than the one he had previously and was promoted during this time. He was also able to coach his daughter's softball team. The children had acclimated to a new school and were getting good grades. Janet became pregnant with baby number five and also helped organize an anti-drunk driving group at the local high school. Jack's parents were doing great as well, but all of this positivity unfortunately would not last.

By 1974, things began to change for the Smurls. It began when Mary Smurl, Jack's mother, suffered a heart attack. This led to the entire family struggling to make ends meet, and whether it was a result of the renovations or something else, something paranormal had begun to manifest and make itself known.

It began when Janet began to hear the voice of her mother-in-law who, shortly after her heart attack, was now at home recovering. Doing what she could to help her, she heard Mary calling out her name and rushed to her aid to help her with anything and everything she could possibly need. The strange thing was, Mary at times would either be unconscious, sleeping, or wouldn't have called for her at all. Attributing this bizarre phenomenon to stress, at first, she writes it off.

However, Mary soon started experiencing her own strangeness. She too, as if the words had come from Janet's mouth herself, would hear her name being called. Only, when confronted, Janet had no idea what she was talking about.

That wasn't all, of course – the stains that had previously been painted over and were thought to be covered, began to seep through yet again. New stains began to appear as well, with several appearing on the hardwood floors of the home.

As the days progressed, the eldest Smurl child soon began to experience the presence, too. She was often woken up in the dead of night, frozen with fear and unable to move. She saw translucent figures standing above her or at the edge of her bed, staring and watching her. Although it wasn't exclusive to the midnight hour, the activity seemed to pick up at night.

Often, when Jack was at work or gone, Janet began to have violent and sickening encounters with a being that she couldn't see. She began to be molested by an unseen force. These interactions left her hysterical, feeling violated and unclean.

Trying to come to terms with what was happening to them, the family's luck continued to worsen. Additional appliances including a TV set went up in flames causing smoke and fire damage to the home on several occasions. Unlike the TV, the other appliances were not plugged in so the family to save money, which makes it all the more mysterious. On top of this, several water pipes which were fairly new after the family had initially renovated the home began to leak, not only causing water damage to the house but adding to their financial woes as well.

The string of bad luck would continue for the Smurls, and by 1977 the activity in the home became much more aggressive. The family's radio began to turn itself on and off, typically at strange hours and almost always when the family was trying to sleep. The sinks in their bathrooms began to turn themselves on, pouring what little money they had left literally down the drain, and their toilets began to flush by themselves. Along with this activity, the sounds of footsteps began to be heard all throughout the house and even from inside the walls. Drawers began to open and close by themselves.

Coupled with these happenings was again the stench of rotting meat, what the family would begin to describe as "the dead smell." Instead of dissipating almost as soon as it was detected like before, in one particular area of the house, the smell would permeate all throughout the house and would linger for minutes or sometimes hours.

Up until this point, besides seeing things being moved, dealing with the stains, pipes, and appliances, Jack hadn't been targeted so to speak by whatever paranormal force was now fully awake within the Smurl residence. But one night, when he was trying to get some sleep after a long day's work, his side of the sheets were pulled from his body and the sensation of dozens of hands touching and grabbing him. This ensured that he not only knew he wasn't going to rest that night due to the sheer terror, but that perhaps his wife was telling the truth.

Shortly after moving into the house, Janet had become pregnant and by this time had given birth to two baby girls, expanding the Smurl family to six children. Not long after the twins were brought home, it seemed like whatever presence had been woken up was making itself known, becoming more aggressive, more vindictive – as if it was jealous or hated the living.

One morning, while the majority of the children were at school or napping and the rest of the adults were out, Janet headed to the kitchen to pour herself a freshly brewed cup of coffee. As she turned around the corner, her blood ran cold. Standing in the middle of the kitchen, with a stain seeming to materialize directly underneath it, was a translucent figure with hollow eyes. Frozen in place upon seeing it, it was as if she blinked and whatever the creature was, was gone.

Was this what was responsible for the multitude of paranormal happenings within their house?

As time progressed, Janet continued to hear her name called when there was no one else there – over, and over, and over again. Strangely, as it was before in the beginning, the voices would often sound like her mother-in-law Mary. Even after double or triple checking sometimes, to make sure she wasn't losing her mind, Mary would be nowhere to be found. She truly was alone.

Other strange things that were heard during this time would be heard from the other side of the duplex. Couples do argue and some fight, that just tends to happen to most unfortunately, but these fights were something else. Jack's parents began to hear yelling, screaming and sometimes even items breaking, coming from the other side of the duplex where Jack and Janet lived. These fights became so violent that not only did they think their marriage was collapsing, but they began to become concerned for Janet and the children's safety.

One night, Jack's father couldn't take it anymore. He walked from their front door to the other side and with the fight still raging, he threw the door open, only to be greeted with silence. The entire family was asleep. Not knowing what to make of the discovery, he simply left, bewildered , but the supposed audio of the fights would continue.

Shortly after the bizarre discovery, Mary experienced something that almost gave her another heart attack. One evening while her husband was still at work and she was alone on their side of the duplex, Mary began to hear her name whispered. It sounded just like Janet, but within earshot or several feet of where she had been. Weirded out, as most of us would be, she began to make her way towards the voice that was calling out to her.

That's when she saw it; standing in her living room, with a stain seeping underneath its feet, was the same translucent being that Janet had claimed she had seen just a short while ago. Terrifyingly, its mouth was mimicking Janet's voice, calling out her name.

Frozen in terror at first, with her heart racing, Mary ran to the door, exited, and immediately went into Jack and Janet's door. She was absolutely petrified with fear. The talks that followed this event in particular led to most of the individual experiences being laid out in the open for everyone to know. They all came to the realization that whatever force was in their house was not friendly.

Shannon Smurl, who was only seven years old during this time, was the next target. One day, as she casually walked through the kitchen and into the dining room, a large, glass light fixture fell and crashed into her, cutting her and raising the alarm bells for the entire house. Again, it seemed like the paranormal being or force hated life and now was possibly trying to end it if the opportunity presented itself. Scared but strapped for cash, they were all seemingly stuck in what was supposed to be their fresh start, but instead was becoming their fresh hell.

Shannon continued to experience strangeness of her own. In her diary and later she recounted that often times she would wake up and find herself floating above her bed – literally levitating several feet above her bed. Some nights while floating she was suddenly thrown across her room and into a wall with so much force that she thought she would be crushed.

The climax of these attacks on Shannon happened one night, when she woke up to find herself floating once again. Only, instead of being let back down or smacked into a nearby wall, her door was flung open. She was thrown out of her room and down the stairs.

Her parents heard this happen and rushed towards the screams of their little girl to find her absolutely hysterical and in pain. Fortunately, she would be okay physically after this event in particular.

Another unfortunate soul that would be targeted in the Smurl duplex was the family's German Shephard, Simon. As seen by Janet, several of the children, and even Jack and Mary on many different occasions, Simon was found floating in the air, confused and concerned.

This new development in activity was not just exclusive to Shannon or their beloved dog. Alongside the intensified attacks on Janet, she too would begin to find herself being woken up, floating in the air. Sometimes, horrifically, without control of her body, she would then also be assaulted.

However, Jack wasn't always gone at this time. Frequently at this point he would be home and sleeping beside her, but he could never seem to wake up. It was as if he was being kept asleep or in a state of paralysis while the events took place.

Coupled along these intense and abhorrent manifestations, came activity that was just plain creepy. Not a day would go by without the family hearing scratching noises coming from within the walls, or deep, drawn-out breaths coming from behind them – feeling the exhale upon their necks, making the hairs on their entire body stand on end.

Jack, at times, after a hard day's work liked to unwind and decompress by watching some TV in the living room. On occasion, he fell asleep to whatever was on before eventually waking back up and making his way to bed. However, this night, he found himself awake and coherent but unable to move, as if he was paralyzed or stuck in some kind of a glue trap, like an insect. Unable to break free, he glanced around the room trying to discover the source of his distress.

It was then that he was met face to face with this being, the demon that seemed to be plaguing their lives. The creature grabbed him from the back and slammed him into the door, repeatedly bashing his head into the hardwood below before disappearing.

After this, Jack didn't watch TV to unwind anymore. As a matter of fact, no one could unwind. They were petrified at whatever was taking place in the house. Unable to afford to move between all the adults and seemingly stuck between a rock and a hard place, scared, and unable to figure out what to do, they began to seek help wherever they thought they could find it.

It was winter and the family, besides their daily duties, spent most of their time indoors. While watching TV one afternoon, they saw an interview with Ed & Lorraine Warren, world renowned paranormal experts and demonologists. Not being particularly religious and unsure of where to turn, they decided to reach out to the couple and were surprised when they made contact. After speaking with them for some time, the Warrens agreed to come to their house to meet in person with the Smurls and to investigate.

Within a week, that's exactly what they did. After an initial meeting with the family, hearing their testimonies in person, and exploring the home, the Warrens decided it seemed genuine and was worth investigating. They began their usual process of bringing in their team for an extended period of time to document and mull over potential solutions for the family. For several months, the documenting team lived with the family and experienced strange activity themselves, such as furniture stacking on top of itself along with several other previously mentioned happenings like the stains and attacks on individual members of the home.

Lorraine finally concluded after having a vision within the house — that they were dealing with a total of four entities. One was that of an old woman, who she believed was not a threat to the family but was simply being held against her will within the home. One was a younger woman who was angry and resentful and could be violent. The other was a man who took the lives of his wife and lover and had been hanged in the same spot a hundred years earlier by a vengeful crowd. The final entity was that of a demon. This demon was not only strong and keeping the other three spirits under its heel of control, but he would use them to strengthen itself and wreak havoc upon the family — to sow discord, anxiety, and fear. All things to which it could feed on and continue to grow ever stronger.

After reaching this conclusion, and having gathered sufficient information, the Warrens spoke to Father Mckenna, who was a Vatican sanctioned exorcist and had worked with them over 50 times on separate cases in the past. He was no stranger to the demonic. However, after his arrival and attempted exorcism, the activity only increased in aggression and hostility. For whatever reason, it was not tied to the home anymore, but rather the family members themselves.

Jack began to experience horrific visions of the creature at work, as did his father. Alongside the continued paranormal activity taking place at their home, their daughter Carin fell seriously ill with a fever that the doctor's couldn't diagnose at the time, and she almost died. Several of the other girls were also visited by the sickening presence at night, as Janet had been and continued to be. The demon also began to physically attack the family more often, causing stinging scratches and cuts on their bodies at random times, as well as deep, bruising bite marks.

Still trying to help the family rid themselves of this creature, fearing the family's continued torment, the Warrens convinced the Smurls to allow a second exorcism to take place. Mckenna again visited and conducted a second exorcism months later in the early Spring. During this exorcism ritual, EVPs were recorded which, when played back after the fact, would reveal multiple entities laughing at and berating them for their efforts. Ed Warren was also choked during this visit and was incapacitated for multiple days after.

Unfortunately, the second exorcism also failed, leading to even more violent manifestations of evil. Trying to get away from it all, even for just a few days, the family went on a camping trip to the Pocono mountains, but the demon followed them there as well. It tormented them wherever they went, allowing for no rest, no decompression, and no peace.

Upon returning to their home following this trip and getting ever more desperate, they decided to reach out to a local TV show called *People are Talking* to see if anyone could possibly help them. They did, however, remain anonymous during their interview. This call for help went unanswered, and the demon seemed to retaliate against them for it. Janet was again hurled against a wall, and Jack experienced something truly terrifying and new.

As he woke up in the early morning to get ready for work before the sun had come up, a light rain tapped the glass of the windows outside. He dressed himself and began to gather his things for his workday departure. Then he came down the stairs and was greeted by a disgusting and horrid creature. Standing in front of the door was a monstrous being whose head almost touched the ceiling. It resembled a horrible amalgamation of a man and a pig standing upright on two legs. It screeched and rushed towards him. As he fell backwards and onto the stairs, hurting his back, the creature stood over him face to face, snarling before it disappeared completely.

This manifestation disturbed and rattled Jack to his core. Although terrified, he still went to work – he still had to provide for the family if they ever wanted to have a chance to escape their hellscape of a home. Janet was woken up a short while later, by a hand reaching up through her mattress and grabbing her from the back of her neck, pulling her towards it and choking her. After this manifestation, horrific snarling noises like that of a pig could be heard coming from inside the walls.

By August of 1986, the Smurls felt that the risk of ridicule did not outweigh the need for their story to reach a wider audience so that somehow, somewhere, somebody could possibly help them be free of their torment. They were soon granted an interview with the Wilkes-Barre Sunday Newspaper. However, instead of someone reading and immediately coming to their aid, their home quickly became a tourist attraction. The press, skeptics, and curious onlookers alike began to visit the house and camp outside of it at all hours of the day and night. Some particularly weird people even came up and stared into the home's windows themselves.

Although previously mentioned, some of their neighbors who had seen and heard strange things coming from the Smurl residence began to turn on them. They believed that the family was concocting some kind of a story to try and make money.

Eventually, however, despite the torment inside and outside of the home now that they were experiencing, the Smurls were contacted by a medium by the name of Mary Alice Rinkman, who offered to meet with them. Upon meeting the family and walking through the home, it was also Mary's conviction that there were four entities within the house – three human spirits and one who had never been human, thus corroborating the Warrens' beliefs about the situation.

She would, however, take things a bit further; she identified the old woman by the name of Abigail, the murderous man as Patrick, and the violent and ill-tempered spirit as Alice, Patrick's wife. The fourth entity, of course, could not be identified by name but it was a very powerful demon indeed.

The press coverage, along with the ridicule and the positive acquaintance of Mary, also pushed the Scranton

Catholic Diocese into action. They offered to take over the investigation.

In the meantime, the Warrens had not given up on the family but rather had reached out to several more priests and had arranged for a mass exorcism to be conducted with four priests taking part, as well as prayer groups. Alongside this, Bishop Mckenna came in for a third and final time and conducted an exorcism on the house for the family. Fortunately, the ritual seemed to work, at least for a time, because following it there were no disturbances for about three months.

However, as winter set in for that year, just before Christmas 1986, Jack again saw the creature that had tormented them for all of those years. This time, however, it beckoned him to allow it to take over. Clutching a rosary in his pocket that had been gifted to him by the church, he prayed as hard as he could. Thankfully, this time the demon vanished, never to be seen again.

However, the putrid smells and violent manifestations returned and continued day in and day out. Frustrated, hopeless, and exhausted, at that point the Smurls had finally saved enough to be able to leave the dreaded duplex on Chase Street. They decided they needed the closest thing to a fresh start as they could get. When they finally did move, they moved to a completely new town, one where the ridicule would not find them.

However, like the terrible pattern shown before, the demon did not seem to be tied to the property but rather the family. The activity started back up almost as soon as they had moved in and laid their heads down to rest in their new home. It took some time, but in 1988 the church finally sanctioned a fourth exorcism, this time at their new residence. This finally seemed to have given the family peace.

There are a few things I would like to mention, however.

From my own personal experience and many other stories I've researched, it seems like renovations, particularly on older homes, can wake up dormant spirits or hauntings. Perhaps this is what happened to the Smurls.

It's hard telling if the assaults were on or multiple demonic entities, but if they did truly exist, how did they get in the home to begin with? My guess is that the collection of negative energy attracts them like moths to a flame. Perhaps they enjoy or feed off human suffering. This would only make sense to me considering they hate humans and refused to bow to them in the beginning, thus leading to the great rift, biblically speaking. Perhaps once they're embedded in one's life, they continue to sow said suffering to exploit and grow stronger. Maybe they're ultimately trying to take the human's life, dragging their soul back with them to hell.

I would also like to mention that scratching on a person and inside the walls, as well as disembodied breathing, are all signs of demonic infestation. For one reason or another, having actually experienced this personally, seeing the manifestation of a pig-like demon or creature, as well as hearing pig like snarling coming from within the walls, is considered to be a serious or incredibly strong sign of a demonic infestation, too.

As far as the initial activity, the seeping through of the stains, the sinks turning on, toilets flushing on their own, and leaky pipes, those initially could be written off as poor skill when the work was initially done. But it seemed like in this story, all of these things were working perfectly fine for months before they all of a sudden began to go wrong, almost at the same time, while also costing the family money they didn't have. Money at that time seemed to be their main issue, along with the paranormal. Perhaps the demon knew and exploited this to add to the misery it was feeding on.

Truly, at the end of the day, the conclusion is yours to make. Was the Smurl haunting legitimate or just another tale concocted for money, or inside the broken minds of the individuals who claimed to have experienced it?

They eventually released a book about all they had experienced called *The Haunted in 1988*. The success of the book is unknown as I couldn't find any records.

What I do know is this: it's extremely important to examine a situation from all angles before just diving into it. Although a place might seem like a fresh new start, it could indeed also be your fresh new hell. Those renovations you think are going to improve your quality of life could awaken something that has been watching and waiting for a fresh host to attach itself to and feed upon, until it can wear it down, rot, and eventually drag it back to the depths from where it came from.

# CHAPTER 5
## THE MONROE DEMON HOUSE

Many homes have been given the title of demon house – many of which I have covered in my investigations – but this house out of all of them has truly earned the moniker. From the time soil was dug up during the Victorian era, a curse seemed to be placed upon the land. When you combine terrible happenings with occult rituals it's truly a recipe for disaster, the results of which have produced a cornucopia of paranormal activity within this now infamous Indiana home.

This is the untold story of the Frightening Monroe Demon House of Indiana.

Information available on this property is scarce at best, but I have done my best to find out as much as I could to try and provide you with the most cohesive picture possible.

What was started as a small log cabin settlement, continued to grow and eventually hit the big time in the late 1880s, where itself and its neighbors entered a natural gas boom resulting in many factories being created during industrialization, factories that produced textiles, glass and other goods. Although natural resources were widely abundant within the ground there, something else seemed to inhabit the soil.

---

Our story begins at the construction site of a rather unsuspecting-looking Victorian home. The year is 1892 and the Berger family who immigrated to the area from Belgium had been successful in their business endeavors, and thus thought a new home in their new country would be the ultimate earthly reward. However, the family's newfound happiness would be all but short lived.

From the time the earth was dug up and the new home erected – within months – John Berger, the patriarch of the Berger family, died from tuberculosis within its walls. Mourning his death, this was far from the last tragedy his family endured moving forward.

Shortly after John's death, a fire mysteriously started in the upstairs level of the house, in time destroying a large portion of the property and the majority of the Berger family met a truly gruesome and terrible fate.

Following the horrific fire that torched what little happiness the Berger family had left, the widow of the family and one surviving child desperately needed a source of income. The widowed Mrs. Berger decided to start renting out rooms in order to make it. There would be various tenants but the most prominent was the Miars family.

The head of the household, a man named Ulysses Miars, was a well-known and respected member of the community. He was known for his kindness, compassion, and for being an all-around amazing family man. But this reputation would also fade.

Shortly after moving into the home, Ulysses slowly began to change. Those who knew him believed that he had made a complete shift in his entire personality within months, so much so that he became unrecognizable not only to his close friends but to his family as well. His kindness, compassion and care all seemed to have been buried. Someone new greeted them each day behind the eyes of Ulysses. He quickly became prone to fits of rage and insanity. This led him to become abusive towards his once beloved family, verbally as well as physically. These new bursts of rage weren't reserved strictly for his family, though; he soon turned on friends and colleagues, too.

This sudden heel turn for Miars led him to losing his job after an altercation at his workplace. Shortly after this, despite how much he had cherished his family before, he stole what was left of his family's money and abandoned his wife and children by skipping town with a newfound mistress. All of which was the polar opposite of the man they thought they knew.

Shattered beyond repair, the Miars family were left with open wounds in their hearts and confusion in their minds. The only differing factor from their life before to what it became, was the fact that they had moved into the house.

With the home claiming the destruction of two families, rumors quickly began to spread locally throughout Hartford City that the house contained some kind of curse. Whether it was upon the property, or the land was uncertain.

The Miars family soon moved out and, due to the rumors, Mrs. Berger was unable to keep tenants to help support her and her surviving child. Thus, she was forced to sell the property at a fire sale rate in order to start somewhere new. What happened to the Bergers is unknown.

With this new ownership, a revolving door of tenants and owners began. As soon as one family moved in, they would almost immediately move out. Again and again this cycle would continue; it would go from being lived in by a family to being rented out and built onto, eventually creating its triplex design that we know today.

Those who had moved in and out often reported experiencing bizarre activity and others simply just didn't say anything, possibly not wanting to come to grips with the reality of what they had been through. This ever-changing list of tenants would continue for decades.

Along with this revolving door of people came a revolving door of peculiar behaviors and practices. Rumors began to circulate in the late 1980s and into the early 1990s that tenants during that time frame were performing occult rituals and ceremonies within the home, especially within the basement. Black magic, rituals, and cere- monies. Those conducting them attempted to harness the negative energy that dwelled there to conjure a demon to do their bidding. Although information is limited, one could assume that perhaps their efforts were successful.

From the mid-90s onward, the strangeness that surrounded the house on Monroe Street only intensified, with new stories coming from new tenants and neighbors alike – stories that this old Victorian home housed a dark and malevolent force. These stories soon began to spread like wildfire. Those who moved into the house typically would only last a year in the home, or less. They often fled in the middle of the night with nothing but the clothes upon their backs, only continuing to solidify that some- thing evil dwelled within the house.

Things got so bad, in fact, that even when the home was abandoned for a time the windows would be blacked out in order to keep people from looking inside. Not because of vandalism problems, but due to so many neighbors and passers-by calling the police claiming that they kept seeing shadowy figures walk around the interior of the Monroe house.

With the home providing a plethora of paranormal evidence and experiences, this soon drew the attention of paranormal scholars and investigation groups from all over the country. This is just some of the activity said to have been experienced by various groups over the years. People have reported a vast number of supernatural happenings, many of which have been caught on film, photo or digital audio recording. These range from aggressive and insulting EVPs to full-bodied apparitions, shadow figures and possibly inhuman manifestations. Mysterious sounds like knocking, banging, and footsteps are common. Doors and cabinets slamming shut with incredible amounts of force.

Most of the activity seems to be centered around the basement, as well as the top floor. The top floor is speculated to be the place where the fire had started that engulfed the Berger family, and the basement was where the alleged black magic rituals took place. In both of these locations, an eerie, shadowy specter of an old, malicious woman is said to attack people.

But just who could this entity be – someone who had previously lived there, or something inhuman cloaking itself in some kind of familiar skin?

Stories of groups panicking and fleeing have become commonplace, too. One anonymous paranormal group in 2014 had such a disturbing experience that they fled, in fear for their lives. They arrived on site at the Monroe house amidst a strong thunderstorm. Unpacking their vehicle, attempting to keep their equipment dry and safe, they made their way inside to dry off and begin documenting whatever they could find there.

As they investigated, asking questions and provoking interaction, recording level by level, the more activity they began to experience. Shadows moved out of the corner of their eyes, bangs, knocking, and cabinets slamming shut could be discerned from the reverb of the thunder outside. But it's when they decided to go down to the basement that their lives would be altered forever.

As they descended the stairs, an eerie cold began to overtake them. As they asked their questions, attempting to catch any activity they could, their flashlights and devices failed. Left with only the enveloping darkness with the occasional flash of lightning coming through the basement windows, something appeared to them that caused them to flee immediately.

Just what or who this apparition was cannot be confirmed. Whatever it was terrified them so much that they fled into the torrential downpour and refused to ever return. When asked for details, even separately, the group has thus refused to discuss the incident further. Whether this is for fear of whatever this thing is/was reentering their lives, or the mere thought is so reality shattering, one cannot be sure. This incident and its aftermath truly makes you wonder just what they could've seen within the dilapidated, damp basement that accursed night.

Investigations would continue with multiple groups coming in and out until a very peculiar discovery took place in 2016, and this discovery would lead to much speculation as to what could've happened within the house. While conducting an investigation for their show *Paranormal Lockdown*, Nick Gross and Katrina Weidman found themselves in the basement and were slowly drawn to the crawlspace of the house. As they traversed in the darkness, what they would find would alter the story forever. Located within the crawl space were human remains – bones buried in a shallow grave.

This not only freaked the entire crew out but prompted them to stop filming and call the police immediately. From here, a full-scale investigation was conducted. The remains were excavated and sent to a local coroner in Indiana for further examination. The bones were indeed confirmed to be human and were at least a hundred years old, possibly older. Following the coroner, they were sent to Indiana University for further testing to determine the age and identification. At this point, the final outcome has not yet been reported – not the age of the individual found or their identity or the potential cause of death. The presumed investigation is still underway.

This put a brief pause on people being allowed to enter the now privately owned home, but that pause has since been lifted, with many more investigations taking place over the years since. With these investigations, even more paranormal activity and increasingly aggressive activity has been reported. These investigations range from the amateur to the professional, from the average joe to YouYubers and famous paranormal teams. Those who have entered the walls of the Monroe Demon House have experienced in addition to previously mentioned activity strange sights, smells, and feelings, demonic snarls, growls, and even full-blown attacks. These have involved scratching, biting, and being shoved. Often times these more intense manifestations are accompanied with aggressive and commanding EVPs where people's names are often used, and windows slamming with so much force that they shatter, leaving fragments of glass all over the floor... just like the fragments left of the lives of the families who once dwelled there.

One previous owner of the home allegedly even jumped out of a window upon being attacked by a demonic apparition that made him dive through the window. Imagine that for a moment. You are so terrified that you would rather risk diving through a window and breaking it, let alone falling however far and injuring yourself out of pure fear and fight or flight, instead of dealing with whatever was rushing towards you. To me, that is bone chilling.

Others who have stayed more recently have also reported puddles of strange liquid throughout the house at varying times, with seemingly no origin. They have horrific nightmares if they manage to sleep. (Why you would ever sleep there is beyond me.) Even strange footprints or paw prints have been discovered multiple times.

With all of these high strangeness manifestations, we must ask ourselves... just what is it that lurks within the Monroe demon house? Could it have been a curse placed upon the land? Something that predated the building of the house? It's certainly possible, in my opinion. To somewhat back that claim up, Native American artifacts such as arrowheads have been found around the property. Nothing significant has been found that would indicate some kind of a curse – no burial grounds or mounds from what I could find.

What if it was a generational or family curse? Again, it's possible but seems somewhat unlikely from what I've researched. The Berger family up until the home was built had great success in their endeavors and for all intents and purposes seemed happy and thriving. Until, of course, they weren't.

Then there's the enigma of the Miars family. Did Mr. Miars lose his mind due to the home? One could certainly conclude that, considering his complete shift in personality. But what was it in particular that caused him to change so drastically? This question and more we may never truly be able to answer. All we can do is speculate.

Then there are the numerous owners and tenants over the decades since the days of the Bergers and Miars, many of them reporting odd and often scary paranormal or poltergeist type activity. Was this activity also taking place when the older families lived there? Or did it start after their departure? If this was the case – if it started afterwards – was it the result of negative events attracting something dark? Or was one of the families or family members involved in the occult?

And speaking of the occult, just who or what were those people in the late 80s, early 90s doing? What kind of black magic or rituals were conducted and were they responsible for conjuring some kind of entity into the home? Or did their practices just make the entire situation much worse?

And did it have anything to do with the human remains that were found in the basement? And if not the black mages closer to modern times, someone in the early 1900s had to have known just who this person was and what happened to them. And, of course, will the identity and cause of death ever be determined for the poor soul whose remains were found within the home?

Will the activity ever cease? Will the origin ever be truly determined? And will the malevolent activity ever stop?

All of these questions honestly may not have answers. Perhaps they're out of our scope of understanding, or perhaps the answers have just simply been lost to the sands of time. But one thing I can say for certain is this:

Given how many people have experienced dark and spine-tingling paranormal activity within this house, and taking into account how long it has been occurring, this is one home that has truly earned the name the demon house. Because a demon is precisely what may just be lurking within its depths.

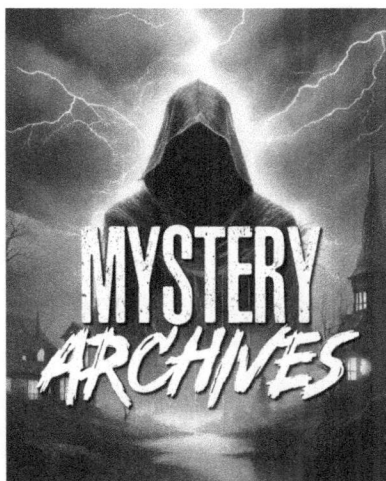

Exploring unexplained phenomena, unsolved mysteries, and bizarre encounters with cryptids, humanoids, and the paranormal. From spine-chilling ghost stories to tales of the demonic, if you're seeking a mystery, you've come to the right place.

Listen & Watch
https://www.youtube.com/@MysteryArchives

# CHAPTER 6
## THE SAN PEDRO HAUNTING

The oldest and strongest emotion of mankind is fear, and the oldest and strongest kind of fear is fear of the unknown. It's what lurks in the shadows that truly frightens most. This case is a strange and terrifying example of a paranormal force crossing the veil between our world and wherever it dwells within the darkness. Its malevolent intent and calculated intelligence scared and affected those who were involved, continuing to haunt them to this very day.

This is the Untold Story of The Terrifying San Pedro Haunting, also known as the Jackie Hernandez Case in California.

---

Jackie Hernandez left her husband in the winter of 1988. Her marriage was rocky to say the least, a domestic drama, a story which is all too common in this world. Working with a limited budget and few belongings, she had to look after her two-year-old son Jamie and unborn second child. The pregnancy should have been a happy development but turned bittersweet due to being over-shadowed by the problems presented by an unhappy marriage.

She soon found a small house located in San Pedro, California that seemed like it could be just what she needed to get back on her feet. Although it would take some time, she was willing to do what she needed to do to get out of her marriage and take care of her children. As the family moved into the home and began to inhabit its walls, what they didn't realize was they already weren't alone.

Jackie later admitted that she had always feared someone breaking into her home, particularly after she started living alone. Upon crossing the threshold of this new house – despite the fact it would be all too easy for a seasoned criminal to break into – that fear was somehow gone. At first, Jackie said she felt a presence, something not of this world, but she felt almost protected and at ease – something she wasn't used to. The presence began to show itself in small, strange ways.

The very first thing Jackie said she ever experienced was when she had friends over. One of her friends was sitting at a table near her in the kitchen and the other on a couch in the living room. As she passed by a desk that held a cupful of pens, although several feet away, they were awestruck when the cup glided by itself across the table it was sat on towards Jackie, and then collapsed to the floor, shattering. Stricken with curiosity as to how it could've happened, they were confused and surprised to say the least. However, not having the answers, this seemingly innocent strangeness became a distant memory before too long.

In February of 1989, the activity seemed to escalate, as the presence Jackie felt began showing its true intentions. Jackie woke up one evening, heading to her children's room to see if they were still asleep. Upon walking into the room, she stopped dead in her tracks. Sitting beside her sleeping son on the lowest bunkbed was a man in a red flannel shirt and jeans. His skin was gray, his face angry. A living, rotting corpse was staring at her son.

She was so scared she couldn't scream, even if she wanted to.

The man glanced at her menacingly, then vanished.

Jackie panicked and called several friends to help her, but they found nothing. This was but the first instance of the frightening specter revealing itself. Several of Jackie's friends and even her neighbor witnessed things they couldn't explain in the following months.

The neighbor, Susan Castaneda, said, "At first when Jackie said she felt something, I didn't really believe her. I thought it was her own confidence in herself. But that was until the manifestations began to show themselves to her, and then to me. I don't know what it is, but I saw it, I smelled it, I experienced it. It touched me, it talked to me, it even visited my house to let me know it was real."

One night, as it stormed outside and rain tapped the glass of her bedroom windows, Susan slept soundly. Yet as she slept, something supernatural was churning like the storm outside the house. She was suddenly startled awake by a massive banging noise in her room.

It wasn't thunder.

Her large, antique lamp on the other side of her bed had somehow moved. It had been thrown into the middle of the room and now laid in pieces. As she made this discovery, a flash of lightning illuminated the room, revealing a man standing before her. His face was like that of a dead person, his eyes angry. Suddenly, as quickly as the room lit up and the illumination dissipated, he was gone. Something peculiar was left in his wake – a putrid, rotting smell.

After the experience Susan had, which would be one of many to come, another friend by the name of Darlene had an experience of her own. She would regularly babysit Jackie's children Jaime and Samantha while their mother was at work. One such afternoon, as the children watched cartoons on TV in the living room, Darlene got up to use the restroom. She stepped back into the hallway and headed towards the small home's bathroom when she was greeted by a voice calling out to her from inside the darkened room.

The intense, spine-chilling voice said, "Don't come back here."

She did as she was told, fearing the unknown entity would become violent if she didn't.

As the days passed, Jackie only became ever more restless. The activity persisted, only becoming more aggressive and more visible. A strange liquid began to drip from the walls and various crevices throughout the house, with no logical origin. Weirded out by this but not knowing what it was, Jackie would clean it up and try to go about her day.

However, the entity was far from finished.

One evening, when placing a storage bin inside of her attic to try and conserve what little space she had, she felt as if she was being watched. To her shock and amazement, she began to see what she would later describe as a floating head, slowly coming towards her. Upon seeing the specter, it picked up speed dramatically. It came at her so quickly she panicked and fell off the chair propping her up to gain access to the attic. Following this incident, she began to hear loud noises emanating from the attic above, coupled by whispers coming from the small access door above her laundry room.

Getting no sleep and reaching her breaking point, Jackie began to get desperate for some kind of help. Her friend and neighbor Susan had recently seen a show on TV of a crew who investigated the haunting of the Queen Mary.

She did some digging and was able to find their phone number.

At Susan's recommendation, Jackie gave them a call. After discussing what she was experiencing, her point of contact passed the information along to the group. She was contacted back, and together they set up a time for them to meet and begin a potential investigation.

The group consisted of a fairly well-known parapsychologist and other professionals in assistive fields. The parapsychologist was Barry Taft who had been involved in over 3000 cases and investigated the case that later become famous for a movie adaptation known as The Entity. A professional camera man named Barry Conrad also joined them. He had previously worked for NBC and ABC, winning multiple awards in his field for his expert work behind the lens. A photography expert by the name of Jeff Wheatcraft completed the main crew, having spent multiple years as a photography expert in New York. He was well versed in debunking photos and was also a well-known heavy skeptic – an important piece when trying to remain scientific in a field such as this.

All three arrived at the San Pedro home for the first time on August 8th, 1989. Upon their initial survey of the home, they unanimously agreed it felt as though there was a massive pressure around them and in their ears. This pressure felt as if they were deep underwater. Alongside this, the home had a very peculiar scent. A foul, rotting smell permeated the air within its walls.

After an initial walkthrough, the crew interviewed Jackie and Susan in the living room, where they were introduced to many of the details of what they both said they experienced. Upon hearing Jackie's account of a disembodied head flying towards her in the attic, Jeff (although not voicing it at the time) didn't believe her. Knowing what they were there to do, he suggested the group at least take a look in the attic to see if they could feel anything.

He volunteered to go first into the attic, thinking it would simply be empty and the lady was spinning a fantasy. As he climbed into the space above the laundry room, flashlight and camera in hand, he began to walk around. The first thing he noticed was the feeling of being watched by something he couldn't see. The feeling was so acute, the hair on his body stood on end. Trying to shake the feeling someone or something was practically breathing down his neck, Jeff began to take photos before descending back to the main level of the house. He snapped one photo, two photos...

Upon snapping the third photo, an invisible force yanked his camera from his hands.

Dumbstruck by what had just taken place, he screamed and ran, descending the attic as quickly as he could. He returned to the rest of the crew, white as a ghost. He took a minute or two to collect himself before working up the nerve to go and retrieve his camera.

As he climbed back into the attic, much more cautiously, he noticed the camera wasn't anywhere near where he had been standing. Instead, the lens was standing up in one corner of the attic and the body was in the completely opposite corner from where it had been pulled from his hands. He retrieved it as quickly as he could and descended yet again.

Jeff later said after this initial experience that he knew – he just *knew* in his soul – that there was something up there.

The group discussed a plan of action and continued to speak with the ladies in the living room, until it was decided Jeff and Barry would go into the attic together to try and record some video of the space. However, every time Barry attempted to take the camera up into the attic, it would shut off. Thinking it was some kind of battery issue, he went back down, only for the camera to come back on. During the troubleshooting process, Jeff was again targeted. He was pushed by unseen hands, so much so that he had to grab hold of a wooden beam in the attic to keep from falling through the entrance.

Upon their return to the main floor, the entire group was startled into silence when a loud banging noise began to come from the far reaches of the attic itself. They hushed each other to listen. Once it finally stopped, the group knew they were experiencing something they couldn't explain and were convinced this was the real deal.

Attempting to photograph whatever could have been making the noise, Jeff partially put himself into the attic to snap photos. He saw multiple flashes of lights, followed by what he would describe as a massive black shadow or presence, moving from side to side.

The crew left for the night shortly after this interaction and planned to return several weeks later. However, shaken by what he experienced, Jeff did not want to participate.

On August 28th, 1989, the remaining crew returned. Things seemed relatively quiet at first, not nearly as active as the initial experience.

That was until about 4am.

Sitting in the kitchen, they began to see a strange liquid pour from inside the cabinets. This was the very same liquid Jackie described to them that she had cleaned up several times before. Since the opportunity presented itself, the crew decided to take samples of the mysterious liquid and sent off to a lab for analysis. As they collected samples from all over the house throughout the course of the night, they tried to determine if there was any potential logical source the liquid could be coming from. However, they discovered no pipes, no trickery. They had no valid explanation as to what could be causing the strangeness.

The results from the lab were bizarre to say the least – the liquid was actually human blood plasma with a high concentration of copper and iodine. The plasma had come from a human male. This stunned everyone and further deepened the mystery of this very unusual haunting.

The crew planned to return after a short time while they examined the things they had captured to try and determine just what could be causing the haunting. In the meantime, Jackie was left alone, or on rare occasion, with a friend. She frequently left voicemails of what she was experiencing on Barry Conrad's answering machine.

Shortly after their second visit, the banging in the attic began again while Jackie was trying to sleep. She sat up, terrified, waiting for it to stop. It ceased, but something new and equally horrifying took its place – the sound of deep, monstrous breathing. This manifestation made Jackie scared for her life and convinced her she couldn't sleep in the house any longer. She became certain she could not live there anymore.

Various members of the crew stayed with Jackie to further investigate, when their schedules would permit. However, one night stood out. It was no ordinary episode – this night was a matter of life and death.

On September 4th, 1989, drained and exhausted, Jackie Hernandez was alone in the home once again. Barry had just left the previous night after capturing additional footage. However, after convening with his colleagues, he discovered a frantic voicemail waiting for him.

Screaming as things broke in the background, Jackie described what happened like this, "Almost as soon as Barry left, things began to go crazy in the house. Items like dishes, knives, and other things were being thrown across the room. It was trying to hurt me. My kids' toys were being levitated, and then being ripped apart before my very eyes."

Even more frightening, as Jackie was leaving the frantic voicemail while the activity surrounded her, her phone line was cut mid cry for help. The crew rushed down to San Pedro, but instead of picking her up and getting her as far away from the home as they could possibly get, Jackie was surprised when the guys rushed inside the home with their equipment.

At first glance, everything seemed to be calm, almost too calm.

Jackie began telling the men among the more chaotic activity she had been experiencing, she again had heard breathing and whispering coming from the attic. Jeff and a colleague named Gary decided they would go up to investigate, despite Jeff feeling not so great about being in the home once again. It had been nearly a month since his initial visit and experiences.

At 12:50am, Jeff and Gary crawled into the attic. Within minutes, Jackie and Barry heard what sounded like three distinct snaps, like someone snapping their fingers. As Barry was holding his camera with both hands and Jackie was standing directly beside him, they yelled to Jeff and Gary that the activity was on the surface level. They asked the men to come back down out of the attic.

Gary, who was closer to the exit, began to make his way towards it and Jeff, who had been in the center of the attic holding his flashlight, approached behind him. Little did Jeff know these steps would be ones he'd never forget.

Before Gary's very eyes and camera lens, Jeff was hoisted into the air and against the ceiling, by a support beam of the attic. He was being strangled by something that neither of them could truly see. As his legs kicked several feet off the ground, he dropped the flashlight. Unable to see, Gary snapped a series of photos to be able to see Jeff. He then ran to his aid to try and free him, before whatever this was took his friend's life.

He found some kind of cord had been tied around Jeff's neck and pulled to the ceiling. The cord had been secured by a bent nail that he actually had to bend straight to free him. Once Jeff was freed, he was dragged as quickly as possible towards the exit as he came to.

Jeff described his experience later, "I remember feeling myself being strangled, and then everything went black. That dark space of time that I lost... I felt so out of control."

Once Jeff was out of the attic, the cord that was noosed around his neck – which had never previously been seen by anyone who had gone into the attic – was found and taken off of him. As Jeff tried to come to terms with what had just happened, Barry, the man behind the camera was attacked next. A surge of electricity from his over-the-shoulder camera shocked him to the point of losing consciousness.

At that point, everyone was terrified and knew they had to leave immediately. Jackie gathered her son and four-month-old daughter, and the rest of the crew began to depart the house as quickly as they could. Jackie's daughter started crying, due to a large red mark on her forehead that came out of nowhere. The activity picked up in the house as they made their way out. Banging noises could be heard coming from inside the house as they all exited shortly after 3am.

In later interviews, Jackie Hernandez would say, "I was in a way forced out by a ghost. But if I would've stayed, I would've been harmed or had a nervous breakdown. I couldn't see a future staying there. I just knew I couldn't stay there."

It wasn't very long after that Jackie made her departure from the house – a permanent one. It would also be the last time the crew and anyone else involved would step foot within the San Pedro home. However, this would not be the end.

In October 1989, wanting to get as far away as she possibly could, Jackie used what little resources she had to move to a modest trailer home 300 miles north of San Pedro, to Weldon, California. Although she still feared the nights, she felt as if whatever presence dwelled within the San Pedro house had been left there. But she would be very wrong.

The following year, in April 1990, one moonlit night, Jackie was woken up by a series of strange scratching sounds coming from inside the small storage shed in her backyard. Thinking it was an animal, she grabbed a flashlight and approached it. As she got to the door and pulled it open, the scratching sound stopped and an all too familiar sense of fear came flooding back. Although she didn't hear anything else going bump in the night, all the hair on her body stood on end just like it had at the San Pedro house.

Just weeks after this development, Jackie would see a large, black mist float through the hallway and towards her daughter's room. Rushing to make sure her child was okay, she passed the threshold of the room and immediately panicked. The comforter her daughter was lying on was on fire. Bizarrely, it looked as though something or someone had touched or sat down exactly in the spot where the burning was. Thankfully, her children were okay after she quickly extinguished the flames and snapped a series of photos as evidence, believing the presence to be back in their lives. The black mist, however, was nowhere to be found.

As a result of the past dealings at the San Pedro house, as well as the resurgence in her new home, Jackie began to suffer horrific panic attacks and almost constant anxiety due to the trauma she endured. She wouldn't be able to breathe when the knocks began at night, and they were always in threes.

Having kept in touch with the guys who had been documenting the San Pedro phenomenon, Jackie updated them on the new incarnation. Never having seen this type of haunting before, the crew wanted to come up and see for themselves if this thing, this entity had indeed followed her to her new home.

It was midnight on Friday, April the 13th when Barry and Jeff arrived. In later interviews Jeff would say, "Many people have asked me, after what you experienced, why on earth would you go following this woman and her ghosts? The only response I could give is that I was compelled to finish this case. I wanted to see it through to the end, to some kind of conclusion."

By this time, Jackie's nearby neighbors had experienced some activity themselves, which only began to take place after Jackie had arrived. In one incident, a couple of her neighbors were moving a new television into their home when the face of an old man with evil eyes materialized in the screen. It was seen by both the husband and the wife moving it.

Word had slowly gotten around and some of the teenage neighbors in the area noticed the unfamiliar van parked outside of Jackie's house that Friday night. After knocking on the door and being informed of what was happening, two teens left and quickly came back with a Ouija board, hoping to assist.

Given the time spent coming up, the desire to make contact and to try and gain some sort of a resolution, and that it was a full moon and Friday the 13th, the crew thought that perhaps this was their best and only opportunity to contact whatever this thing was and to try and illicit a response, and a response they would get.

As they placed the board upon a table that all of them could sit around, the atmosphere was icy cold. At first nothing happened, the board sat there idle. But within minutes, the entire table began to violently shake. The planchet began to move around the board and answer questions so quickly, all they could do was write down letters to try and decipher what it said. The candles surrounding them flickered as if people were running around the room, creating some kind of vortex.

They asked who the entity was, and it told them. He was a man who had been murdered, held underwater and drowned in San Francisco Bay in 1930.

They asked how many spirits walk the earth.

It replied, "Phantoms fill the skies around you."

Jeff then asked it, "Why are you targeting me? Why do you hate me?"

It replied, "You have the likeness of my killer."

They then asked, "Who in this room do you harbor hatred for?"

The board then spelled out Jeff's name.

Within seconds, Jeff himself was picked up multiple feet into the air and thrown into the wall behind his chair. This violence concluded the session. Jeff came to minutes later with an injured back and everyone exited the trailer to try and make sense of the ordeal. As daybreak arrived, it felt as if the presence had weakened or retreated back into the shadows of the night.

Days after the unearthly encounter, Barry decided to take the information he gained and visit The News Pilot, the local newspaper there in San Pedro. He wanted to look through old articles to see if he could verify what the specter had told them. He soon found an article dating back to March 25th, 1930, where the body of a man named Herman Hendrickson had been discovered. Police believed he had been the victim of foul play due to a compound fracture in his skull. However, due to a lack of evidence, his death would ultimately be ruled accidental. Herman Hendrickson was a seaman who worked upon a lumber company vessel known as The Astoria.

Convinced he was onto something, Barry took photos of the cord that had been tied around Jeff's neck in the San Pedro house to the local docks to ask around. Upon speaking to an elderly career fisherman, he was told that the knot was a Bowline knot, a very common knot that has been used on the seas for hundreds of years. It was as common now as it would've been in the 1930s and prior. Whoever tied it had been connected with the ocean in their profession.

Given the resurgence of the supernatural in her new home, Jackie's patience was paper thin. She decided in June of 1990 to move once again, in hopes of leaving the entity behind for good. She relocated back to San Pedro, moving into a small apartment home on 7th Street.

Not wanting to take any chances, she had a local priest come in and bless her home before she and her family would live there. But again, horrifically, it had moved with her. From the very first night, the same phenomena began to rear its ugly head. From lights flickering, objects moving on their own and balls of lights materializing and moving throughout the room, Jackie was once again plagued by an ethereal force. She wasn't the only one.

Every time the guys would return from a separate investigation, a photography shoot, or anything in between, they were met with odd happenings. The first, and one of the more worrisome things to happen, was their gas burners turning themselves on and igniting. Following this continuous show of power, it began to rearrange and move objects such as photographs. To scale in intensity in the weeks to come, it broke multiple windows and began to place furniture upside down.

It eventually reached a crescendo, a blitz of violent and vulgar displays of power. About 50 different items were moved, with Gary, Jeff, and Barry as witnesses. In the middle of the action, in an effort to communicate once again, a letter and pen were placed in the middle of the stove. In response, the burners turned on by themselves and the letter ignited within five minutes.

The entity, whatever it was, wanted them to know it was there, making it clear that no home was truly sacred. Any lingering doubt had been completely erased.

When the case initially began in 1989, no one could've predicted the longevity or persistence of the paranormal phenomena that was to take place, nor how many people it would affect. Today, Jackie Hernandez still experiences minor bouts of spirit activity, but things have long since calmed down from the days of 1989 and through the 1990s. Thankfully for her now, she is able to live a relatively normal life, although her fear of what could be lurking in the darkness still sits in the back of her mind.

Just what caused the spirit to haunt the home in which Jackie found herself in San Pedro?

If it truly was a drowned and tormented soul who harbored hatred as it claimed to be, why would it find a residence over 400 miles away to haunt? And why would it pick Jackie of all people, or could it have been anyone at that specific time? Could it have been the fact that she was vulnerable, or something else?

She also claimed to have never opened any sort of doors, although most of the time that is the way these entities find their way into our world. But perhaps later on, when they asked and received their answers via a Ouija board, they allowed the spirit to become more present.

It bothered other people, like the friends and neighbors of Jackie, and followed Jackie to multiple residences. Perhaps it was strengthened through this process, considering for a time the manifestations became stronger.

Although many people consult a religious leader like a priest to try and cleanse a home or rid themselves of these kinds of entities, why didn't that work when Jackie moved into the final apartment? Could the entity have perhaps attached itself to her?

Or, and although there is no evidence to support this, could her husband or a relative unhappy with the divorce have placed some kind of hex or curse upon her? Just some food for thought as to how she found herself in this position.

With these many questions, we still find ourselves with fewer answers than we'd like when it comes to the now infamous case known as the San Pedro Haunting. However, one thing is for certain – these things do exist and whether you believe based on what you've seen or learned or you're a hardened skeptic sometimes it takes the other world staring you directly in the face to convince you otherwise and your fear, your vulnerability can attract and feed the things that go bump in the night and perhaps fear of the unknown is a well-placed fear indeed.

# CHAPTER 7
## ANNABELLE

A young woman is elated to receive the birthday gift of a doll from her mother, believing it to make a wonderful companion. However, when the doll begins to move on its own and reveals its malevolent nature, it will take the expertise of renowned demonologists and priests to help free them from the entity that now infests their lives.

Will they make it out alive, before it's too late?

This is the untold story of Annabelle, the demonic doll of Connecticut, and this story just may make you think twice about your keepsakes.

———

Our story begins in 1970. Twenty-five-year-old Deirdre Bernard had recently moved into her first apartment with her two friends, an engaged couple named Lara Clifton and Cal Randell. Her mother bought her a gift for her birthday, hoping it would keep her daughter's spirits up and spread joy to her new home as she pursued her education in nursing. Deirdre adored the gift, delighted by its rosy red cheeks and matching hair, which made it a cheerful companion for her new chapter in life.

Shortly after admiring her new doll, she placed it on her bed with its arms and legs out. For the next several days, it became routine for Deirdre to come home from her studies, spend time with the doll, and then place her back almost in the exact same position with its arms and legs out on her bed.

Oddly enough, after the first several days of this new routine, the young woman began to notice something wasn't quite right. Every morning, she laid her doll back on her bed before heading to school, with its arms and legs stretched out. Yet every night upon her return, she found the doll in different positions. Sometimes the doll's legs were crossed, other times its arms. As the days went on, it even started to be seen in different parts of her room, often times with its arms pointed outward.

Deirdre's room was not its only occupied space. The doll began to be found in various positions all over the apartment. Deirdre wasn't the only person to witness the bizarre manifestations. Her two roommates, Lara and Cal, bore witness to them as well.

One evening, Deirdre returned home with her roommates, fellow trainee nurse Lara and her fiancé Cal. Upon opening the door to their apartment, they found the doll kneeling before them in a chair, facing the door as if it had been waiting for them to return. This scared everyone, but especially Deirdre because she knew for a fact, as per her routine, she placed the doll on her bed that very morning. It inexplicably moved on its own.

To try and make sense of it all, they moved the doll and tried to reposition it back into its original kneeling stance, the same one they saw when initially walking through the door. Each time they tried to replicate the position it proved impossible, due to the design of the doll. The movement of the doll as well as their inability to replicate the position left the trio at a loss for words. The only conclusion they could draw from the situation was that some kind of force was manipulating the doll.

Deirdre placed the doll back in her normal position on her bed for the night, but that experience was far from the last all of them bore witness to.

Just several days following the previously mentioned occurrence, a new phenomenon began to manifest. Little notes written in pencil on parchment paper began to be found randomly throughout the apartment, at random times. The messages included phrases such as "help us" or "help Cal." Despite the messages' urgent requests for help, no one was able to figure out just what they were referring to – none of them were experiencing an urgent situation, including Cal. Weirder still, none of them kept parchment paper or pencils. That realization further deepened the mystery that was unfolding before their very eyes.

At first, they believed someone was possibly breaking into their apartment to play pranks on them. In order to check if that was the case, Deirdre and Lara began leaving marks around the windows and doors that would reveal if they'd been disturbed. They also rearranged their furniture in an effort to ensure that if anyone was entering their apartment unannounced, they would leave a trace.

Later that night upon their return from their studies, none of the furniture had been disturbed, nor had any of their marks. Yet the doll had moved rooms. Frightened and perplexed at that point, the trio tried to come up with some potential solutions. As they individually gave it thought, day in and day out, the doll continued to move of its own accord.

One day, the three returned, as per their routine, to find the doll in another part of the apartment, yet again. This time, something was different – they found it sat with some kind of liquid on its hands. Upon a closer look, they were even more frightened because the liquid appeared to be blood. The blood was all over the doll's hands, and three distinct dots of blood were also on its chest.

Terrified, the three sat in the living room and tried to figure out some kind of game plan for how to handle the paranormal situation they found themselves in. Deirdre grabbed a phone book from the cupboard and began flicking through the pages as the group talked. One of her fingers finally rested on a physic medium's number. During the brief call, they explained that they had been experiencing ghostly activity within their apartment, but they did not inform her about the doll specifically.

She arrived the following day to see what she could do to help. As she walked through the apartment, she explained to Lara and Deirdre the spirits she felt inhabited the building. The ladies eventually made their way to Deirdre's room where the doll sat, and they asked what the medium felt regarding the doll. Upon examining it, the medium said she felt a strong presence surrounding the object and informed the two that she would need to conduct a seance around the object to discover more information.

The seance was agreed to, and as the ritual was conducted around the doll, the medium began to divulge information to Lara and Deirdre. She claimed she had channeled the spirit of a seven-year-old little girl named Annabelle Higgins. She said Annabelle used to play in the area long before the houses and apartment buildings were there, back when all that existed were fields. Many innocent and happy hours were passed there until suddenly, they ended. Annabelle was confused as to what had happened to her, to which the medium interpreted to be her death. Since her death, the child had wandered the place she was the happiest – the fields.

Once the apartments were built upon them, the halls became a lonely place for her to haunt. With the lifestyles of most modern people requiring work most of the time, Annabelle had no one to play with. But then, one day, two young women brought with them a playful looking doll.

Finally, she had something to play with again. More so, she had the comfort of two young women who she believed would be more empathetic and accepting of her and would allow her to play with them.

Through the vessel of the medium, Annabelle asked if she could live in the doll and be with Deirdre and Lara. Touched by the young girl's story, the two women agreed. Following the seance, they named the doll Annabelle in the young girl's honor. Convinced that they were sharing a space with Annabelle, they began to treat the doll as a living, breathing person. It was no longer a lifeless doll, but a young and lonely little girl. It was a truly nice gesture from the two of them; however, agreeing to have Annabelle inhabit the doll and stay with them was when the haunting truly began.

Regardless of the two ladies' compassion, Cal was not so convinced. He sensed something was very off about the entire situation and believed that no good would come from it. He thought the doll could possibly be some kind of trickster or conduit disguising its true intentions.

In the weeks following the séance, Cal began to feel ill most times of the day with no rational origin. Every single night, he suffered horrible nightmares. Those experiences culminated with Cal waking up one night to find Annabelle gliding over his body. Before he could react, the doll's hands were on either side of his neck, strangling him. Its large, void-like eyes stared into his as it sought to steal his life. As hard as he pushed against the doll, it did not budge.

In a later interview, Cal would describe the event, "While I was lying there, I saw myself wake up. Something seemed wrong to me. I looked around the room, but nothing was out of place. But then, when I looked down toward my feet, I saw the rag doll, Annabelle. It was slowly gliding up my body. It moved over my chest and stopped. Then it put its two arms out. One arm touched one side of my neck, the other touched the other side like it was making an electrical connection. Then, I began to be strangled. I was writhing and trying to push the doll off my chest, but I might as well have been pushing on a wall because it wouldn't move."

Just as he felt himself slipping out of consciousness, he pushed back with every fiber of his being and finally threw the doll away from him. Cal was terror-struck but relieved. However, this was far from the last time Annabelle sought to destroy.

One night, when Deirdre was still out of the apartment, Lara and Cal were spending time together in the living room. This relaxing time was abruptly interrupted by a loud bang emanating from Deirdre's room. The couple, confused as to what it could be, rushed to find the source. Cal headed in first and threw the door open, expecting to see someone.

To their surprise, they were only met with the icy gaze of Annabelle. She stared at them from the floor, as if she had been tossed aside by someone. Cal walked over to the doll and went to pick it up.

Suddenly, he dropped Annabelle and screamed in pain. The young man writhed in agony as white-hot slashes lashed his chest. A small pool of blood began to form in the middle of his shirt as he frantically darted towards the door. Lara was paralyzed with fear as her boyfriend was attacked by something neither of them could see.

The two ran out of the bedroom and back to the living room as fast as possible, praying to God that the force wasn't pursuing them. When they reached the sofa, Lara pulled up Cal's blood-soaked shirt to find several large gashes on his chest that looked like claw marks. It was becoming increasingly clear that Annabelle sought to harm them.

They informed Deirdre what happened while she was gone when she arrived back at the apartment. The three, unsure of what else to do, contacted a local Catholic priest for help. He in turn requested permission to help from his superiors who then passed on the information to paranormal investigators, Ed & Lorraine Warren.

The Warrens were intrigued by what was allegedly taking place and decided to pursue the case in hopes of helping the young trio. Upon arriving at their apartment, they heard each person's testimonies and observed how the space felt, as well as the doll itself. The Warren's believed the happenings to be a result of a heavy demonic infestation. They believed the demon didn't specifically haunt just their apartment, but the building itself and the land around it. It saw the doll as a way in.

The seance essentially allowed the demon to communicate directly with them to be invited into their lives. All those present and taking place in the ritual were highly vulnerable spiritually and this opened them up to manipulation from the entity. It spun a false narrative that it was instead the spirit of little, lonely Annabelle. Following the seance, Deirdre and Lara paid credence to the doll instead of ignoring it, which only fed the demon more energy. It then continued to feed off of them by manipulating their caring and maternal emotions. The women were powerless to resist feeling sorry for the little girl who just wanted to play and be cared for. Once the women accepted the demon into their lives, they and everyone around them became fair game. The entity no longer had to masquerade itself; it was free to unleash its true form.

The couple sensed the demon was very powerful. Given how strong it had continued to grow and infest their lives and given its proclivity to violence, if left unchecked, it would have probably tried to kill one or all of them within the next several weeks. After explaining the gravity of the situation they were facing, the Warrens reached out to a priest they often collaborated with on demonic cases. Father Everett agreed to come and bless the apartment in an effort to weaken or expel the demon.

Father Everett conducted the blessing and departed. However, the Warrens warned the group that if the blessing hadn't driven the demon out, it was severely weakened but could potentially come back with a vengeance. Believing the doll to be the conduit, at

Deirdre's request, the Warrens took Annabelle with them when they left. Deirdre, Lara, and Cal were thankfully free of the demonic entity that had plagued their lives.

However, the Annabelle story is far from over.

The Warrens' problems seemed to begin as soon as Annabelle was stuffed into Ed's briefcase. As the couple headed home, they began to experience issues with their vehicle, which almost resulted in multiple head-on collisions. The demonic entity caused the power steering and brakes to fail, and even the engine to stall.

Once they were able to finally get back home, the doll was placed within the Warrens' home office, specifically within Ed's chair. In the days to come, the Warrens began to witness the doll manifesting paranormal activity within their very house. The doll was seen levitating on several occasions and began to frequently teleport to different rooms. The same little notes written with pencil on parchment paper began to appear with the all too familiar phrases like "help me" and now, "help *us*."

On top of this, one evening while she was alone, Lorraine began to hear what she described as, "loud, rolling growls that reverberated within the walls, throughout the entire house."

Following this night, the Warrens were visited by Father Daniel Mills, a Catholic Priest the couple were working with. Upon inquiring about their dealings with the doll, the priest made the mistake of picking up Annabelle and telling her, "You are nothing but a rag doll and you can't hurt anything."

While the priest laughed, Ed warned him to never touch or say anything like that to the doll ever again. As he prepared to leave, Lorraine warned the priest to please drive carefully. Her clairvoyance revealed to her an impending tragedy involving a young priest.

Appreciating her concern but writing the situation off, Father Mills departed the Warren residence. A few hours later, he was involved in a near fatal car accident which totaled his vehicle after his car's brakes mysteriously failed.

Upon receiving the news that the priest was hurt but would survive the accident, the Warrens decided to lock Annabelle away, in hopes that she would never be able to hurt anyone ever again. They doused her in holy water and placed her within a blessed glass case. A blessed crucifix was also placed on the outside of the box and warning signs asking anyone who may come across the doll not to touch it. The doll was then placed in their occult item collection.

Although Annabelle was sealed away in hopes that she would no longer harm anyone, her power still seems to affect those who have visited her. After Ed's passing, Lorraine often described Annabelle in interviews as one of the most malevolent objects she had ever encountered. Besides numerous bouts of bad luck, some people were said to have encountered death as a result of meeting her.

Numerous people are alleged to have lost their minds and end up in psychiatric care for the rest of their earthly lives.

One day, a young man visited the Warren's museum and clearly didn't think things through. He went up to and challenged the doll, wanting the worst of whatever it had to offer. He had driven to the museum with his girlfriend on his motorcycle. Upon their departure, three hours into their trip home, the man lost control of his vehicle and hit a tree at very high speeds. He died almost instantly due to the impact. His girlfriend, on the other hand, survived but would remain hospitalized for over a year.

Was this particular instance coincidence, or the demon inhabiting the doll inflicting exactly what it had to offer?

Although the Warrens did explain how the demon came into the doll, it elicits a deeper quandary – one that we've seen reoccurring multiple times over our various covered haunted objects. That's to be very careful how much attention, and dedication you give an object. Because depending on your spiritual state and location, that imbuement could potentially open a door or create a vessel for something malicious to make its way in. I also know that the Warrens are controversial figures, now even in death. But regardless, they are integral to many of the paranormal stories we have and will have covered.

But what do you think? Was Annabelle truly possessed? Was the whole case legitimate or a hoax?

And with these questions, you may find yourself wondering where the Annabelle doll is today. Annabelle remains sealed in the same cabinet she was placed in 50 years ago. Ed and Lorraine's daughter, Judy Spera, and her husband, Tony, continue to hold the torch for the Warrens and their work. Annabelle is on display for all to see at the Occult Museum.

If you choose to visit, if you happen to find yourself staring into her big, dark eyes, just know that if you stare too long into the abyss, the abyss just may stare back at you.

# CHAPTER 8
## THE EXORCISM OF ANNALIESE MICHEL

When a young woman began to experience horrific visions during her waking life, she sought help from her parents. Believing the matter to be spiritual, they consulted a priest who tried to drive multiple demons out of her body. Ultimately, the exorcisms failed. It proved to be one of the most compelling and yet controversial cases of the 20th century, possibly ever. This is an exploration of the life and death of a young woman named Annaliese Michel and the six demons that supposedly took her. This is the untold story of the exorcism of Annaliese Michel.

*Disclaimer: Whether this is a true case of demonic possession or the result of malpractice due to religious extremism is not up for me to decide. I will simply present the case as chronologically accurate and full of detail as I can, and that conclusion is ultimately up to you.

German citizen Josef Michel served in the military during World War III and was thankful to return to his family's small village following his imprisonment by the Americans after his release in late 1945. Having seen the horrors and ravages of combat, he thanked God that his small village of approximately three thousand souls hadn't been attacked during foreign army occupation or the devastating air raids that leveled most major cities in Germany.

He was reunited with his family and took a job within his family's business. During that time, he met a local girl named Anna. Within two years, the couple married. They went on to have four daughters who they raised to be religiously devout, attending Mass twice a week.

Anna Elisabeth Michel was born on 21 September 1952 in Leiblfing, Bavaria, West Germany. She went by Annaliese, a combination of her first and middle name. Annaliese was a very shy and sickly child growing up. Although frequently sick, she was known for being very sweet, though she usually kept to herself and her studies while at school.

All went relatively well for Anna, until she turned sixteen years old. Shortly after her birthday, Annaliese fainted in front of her younger sister. Upon her sister calling her name and poking her arm, she came to. She believed that she was just exhausted from studying too much and decided to lay down for the night. That night was when her torment began.

Shortly after the clock struck midnight, Annaliese woke in a panic. A giant force, as she would later describe it, was holding her down on the bed. She felt the area around her body indent, as if a very large person or creature was sitting on top of her. This entity then began to press on her stomach, causing her to urinate. Panicking and unable to breathe, the poor woman called out to God in a desperate attempt to stave off whatever the thing was. Convinced that she was dying, she pleaded for freedom.

Upon the nearby church clock tower sounding the quarter hour, it was all over – all pressure ceased, as if the attacker was blown away. Whimpering in terror, Michel changed her linens and barely slept that night. She informed her mother the following morning that she felt very ill and was exhausted, so her mother allowed her to stay home from school that day.

Nearly one year later, on August 24th, 1969, the invisible attacker decided to strike again. Just as before, she blacked out earlier in the day. Later that night, right after midnight, she felt the familiar but terrifying large force begin to hold her captive yet again. She was unable to breathe and unable to call for help. Again, she was freed by the tolling of the church clocktower bell fifteen minutes later.

She informed her mother of this second incident. Her mother, unsure of what was happening to her poor daughter, decided to take her into the family physician, a man named Dr. Vogt. At the recommendation of Dr. Vogt, they boarded a train to Aschaffenburg to meet with a neurologist by the name of Dr. Siegfried Lüthy.

Dr. Lüthy ran a variety of tests that day, all of which came back negative. Unsure of the results, he asked them to return on August 27th for a follow up appointment and more tests. One of these sequential tests was an EEG which recorded normal alpha type brain activity. Coming up empty handed yet again, the doctor still had to account for the convulsive episodes his patient was experiencing. He diagnosed her with temporal lobe epilepsy and placed her on a drug known as Zentropil, an anticonvulsant.

This seemed to work for a time, but as 1969 progressed, Annaliese became very sick. In December, she contracted pneumonia, which would be further complicated by a tuberculous infection. She became too ill to further her studies and was forced to drop out of school.

She remained in her bed back at home until January of 1970. Her condition still did not improve, so she was transferred to the hospital in Aschaffenburg in February. From there, she was placed in a sanatorium in Mittelberg, Austria, one that specialized in bronchial and lung disease. She made some improvement, but had other issues diagnosed.

When spring came, she longed to go home to see the beautiful, lush hills of her village instead of the jagged and ominously gray mountains that surrounded her. Unfortunately, she was not permitted to leave yet – her condition still needed to improve. Especially with the new diagnoses of cardiovascular and circulatory problems.

However, the all too persistent and familiar force came to plague her yet again on June 3rd, 1970. The same massive, paralyzing entity would grip her with its cold, unseen hands. That time, Annaliese tried everything she could to free herself. In her desperate attempts, a lone scream finally managed to tear loose from her lips. That scream was heard by the night nurse and the young doctor who was on duty, both of whom rushed to her aid. As the two entered the room, the specter released its grip on Michel.

By this point, the commotion had woken up the other girls in the sanatorium. Michel was assisted with changing her pajamas and bedding, and she tried to sleep under nurse supervision for the night. The following morning, the girls' gossip reached a fever pitch. They began to speculate if Annaliese had previously had a head injury, if she had water on the brain or a number of other rumors. Annaliese didn't pay much attention to them. She became withdrawn and was still weak from the previous night's episode. She was more concerned with what was going on with her health.

As the day progressed and dusk settled on the horizon, while the other girls were headed to the cafeteria, Annaliese opted to stay in her room, stare out the window, and say her evening rosary. The mountains which once appeared massive and foreboding appeared more beautiful, their peaks glistening pink and violet as the sun set behind them. As she prayed, the voices of the returning girls seemed louder than usual.

One of the girls approached her as she was admiring the view and praying, asking her if she was alright. She then commented on her blue eyes being black.

Annaliese, unsure what to make of this, shook off the girl's remarks and went on to finish her rosary.

The following day, she was sent to another specialist who would attempt to figure out just what was going on inside her head. After a day's worth of tests, including EEGs, they once again found no evidence of anything being wrong. However, with her now documented history of epileptic seizures, specialist Dr. Kehler prescribed a new anticonvulsant drug.

Upon returning to the sanatorium, Anneliese began to experience a new and terrifying manifestation. In her normal, waking life she saw a horrible, demonic looking creature seemingly stalking her. It appeared on the mountains, throughout the corridors, and in her room. Upon seeing its gnarled face, she would always fall to her knees and beg the Virgin Mary for her grace to make the visions go away.

After six more weeks at the sanatorium, she was examined once again by a physician who ran more tests. As before, she was found to not have any abnormalities in her brain scans. With this final inconclusive assessment, she was finally allowed to return home to her family.

Her return home was happy at first, being back in her own bed surrounded by familiar faces, yet Michel found herself worrying about going back to school, readjusting, and of course, her persistent health issues.

She did end up returning to school to finish her studies, this time visiting multiple doctors all throughout the year to monitor her health. She had several more seizures, although seemingly not as severe as the ones previously experienced. Although those appeared more minor, she was still experiencing horrific, disfigured visions.

Annaliese shared this with her mother and, after time and time again of the doctors not finding anything abnormal about her, Anna began to think that something supernatural was taking place. One evening, the two parents discussed this matter in particular. Anna tried to convince her husband that what plagued their daughter was of the devil. She told him that Annaliese had been seeing horrible, twisted faces all throughout the day and night, sometimes in the mirror or looking out the window. Other times, they would be staring in through the window at her, or through the faces of others.

One vision in particular that Annaliese relayed to her mother disturbed her so much that she had to share it with Josef. Annaliese told her upon seeing the statue of the Virgin Mary on the mantle in their living room, her eyes turned black, a hideous grin appeared on her face, and her small, delicate hands began to twitch, morphing into thick, grotesque claws.

Seeing the sincerity in his wife's eyes, Josef went silent for a few minutes before deciding the family should ask for guidance through prayer.

With school finally finished for Annaliese before university, a summer trip was in order. After consulting with the doctors about his daughter's condition and discovering her depressive thoughts that she had shared with them, Josef decided to take his daughter to the shrine of San Damiano in Italy, in hopes of not only aiding her spiritually but mentally as well. The shrine had been created by a woman named Rosa Quattrini who experienced multiple miracles and received messages from the Virgin Mary, including to have the shrine built. Later becoming known as Mamma Rosa, she worked alongside Padre Pio for many years.

In due time, with the assistance of a teacher, they organized a trip to the shrine and took a bus there through the Italian countryside. Upon their arrival amidst the beautiful vineyards that surrounded the location of the garden in which the shrine was located, a dark presence enveloped Annaliese.

Surrounding the shrine was an open space which allowed pilgrims to kneel and pray. A small crowd was present as Annaliese approached the shrine at the insistence of her father. She felt like she couldn't approach the holy mother. She began to walk around the shrine in a wide arc, her feet began to burn as if walking on hot coals. All of the people she glanced at, although in a praying position, were gnashing their teeth, their faces again distorted and awful. This is where she began to really first display her aversion to holy objects such as medals of saints, statues, and insignia that represented Jesus. Those present couldn't help but notice how strange the young woman was behaving.

Upon heading back onto the bus, the teacher, a woman named Frau Hein, asked what was going on with her. Annaliese expressed her will was not her own and someone else was manipulating her.

Almost as soon as those words left Michel's mouth, her personality completely changed. In a voice that sounded like a man's, Annaliese began to belittle Frau Hein, making fun of her for being unsure of herself. She then snatched a blessed medal off of her neck.

Frau Hein, Josef, and others present on the trip began to smell a stench exuding from Annaliese that they had never experienced before. The smell of fecal matter and something burning permeated the bus.

After their visit to San Damiano, Annaliese seemed to feel quite well despite what had taken place, but this only lasted for about two weeks. She was set to attend college but felt that she was in no condition to do so. She complained to her mother that she was horribly depressed and continuously plagued by these horrible faces.

Believing it to be a result of her daughter's seizures, Anna made an appointment for her with Dr. Lüthy. Several days later, they determined she'd been seizure free between appointments and another EEG indicated her brain was indeed normal.

However, in what had become a reoccurring event, the nonreligious Dr. Lüthy belittled Annaliese for telling him she saw horrible visions on a near daily basis. He believed she was an overly superstitious Catholic girl. That would be the last time she saw Dr. Lüthy and the last time she would mention the demons to any medical professional.

Despite being cleared to head to university, Annaliese was reluctant. Becoming more depressed and withdrawn, Annaliese was confronted by her mother. Anna reminded her daughter she wanted to be a teacher her entire life and now that the opportunity was there, she wasn't taking it. Annaliese explained she was depressed, empty, and tired. The drugs were not helping her; the demons and their manifestations were only getting worse.

Still considering her daughter's issues to possibly be spiritual in nature, Anna arranged for her to begin meeting with priests in an effort to aid her. The two priests who received letters from both Anna and Annaliese were Father Herrmann and Father Alt. After reading the letters, their interest was piqued by the descriptions of what poor Annaliese was experiencing.

Curiously, Father Alt began to feel very ill seemingly out of nowhere. He retired back to his dormitory room for the night to try and sleep it off. Shortly after the clock struck midnight, Father Alt awoke soaked in a cold sweat. A storm raged outside, lightning illuminating the room around him. As he lay in his bed, feeling awful, he began to pray. However, as he prayed, he felt something or someone press on his bed, as if they had walked onto it.

The terrified priest jumped off of his bed and began to pray out loud. As the words left his mouth, a horrendous, burning smell began to fill his room. Father Alt rushed out his door and into his hallway, his vision narrowing and his color perception changing as he rushed down the stairs, headed to the exit door of the building. Within the shadows cascading on the walls and the stained glass surrounding him, horrible, distorted faces began to reveal themselves. Father Alt now knew what he was dealing with – he was dealing with very evil forces indeed.

He rushed outside into the rain, falling to his knees, gripping his rosary as he attempted to catch his breath. He eventually returned back to his room once he felt that the force had passed. However, the scent of burning fecal matter still filled the entire parish. Even the following day, it was still there and was experienced by all the priests and staff.

This event furthered the interest in Annaliese's case and further motivated the priests to act quickly, fearing that the young woman was indeed being affected by the demonic. Father Alt began to meet with Annaliese when he could, accommodating her school schedule. She seemed to be doing fairly well, despite still seeing the manifestations most days.

She began classes on November 1, 1973. Going to lectures day in and day out while seeking various churches and chapels to relax and pray in, she remained a diligent student. Her life, despite the awful manifestations that bothered her still, was about to change in an unexpected way.

At the end of November, Annaliese would meet a fellow student by the name of Peter. He was very shy like herself but became friendly and outgoing when she got to know him. The two shared many classes together and would soon fall in love. Several weeks into the relationship, however, Annaliese told Peter to stop seeing her, fearing that when and if the demons came back, he wouldn't want her. Despite what his new girlfriend told him, Peter denied this and refused to leave her side.

Michel went in for a checkup evaluation, where she had yet another EEG. Only this time, the doctor administering the EEG, a woman named Dr. Schleip, found patterns of epilepsy. Finding such patterns for the first time was a significant discovery. As a result of this, Dr. Schleip changed Annaliese's medication to another anticonvulsant drug known as Dilantin, in hopes that it would improve her condition.

Following this appointment, Peter and Annaliese continued their relationship, and Annaliese confided in Peter more of what she was experiencing with the demonic figures and faces that plagued her. Peter had also become aware of the awful stench that seemed to follow her, especially when she was experiencing these supposed hallucinations. He wanted her to join him in meeting his family and friends, but Annaliese refused, worrying they may not be as understanding as Peter.

Michel ultimately expressed that she did have moments of clarity where she felt as herself but every so often the devils would reappear. Despite her taking her medication daily, the faces remained. Coupled with the faces, she again began to experience headaches.

Father Alt, checking in on her with the local bishop there on campus, discussed her complaints and persistent ailments, despite her taking her medication every single day. He arranged to have Annaliese meet him in a nearby town for the two to pray together. Peter took her to the appointment and was surprised by how quickly she seemed relieved after the two prayed. Although very skeptical, Peter began to believe in the possibility it was some kind of spiritual issue.

Following this meeting Annaliese's depression would return. She told Peter the clanking of knives and forks sickened her, that the demons wouldn't let her eat. Coupled with her losing weight and becoming ever more reclusive, other witnesses to the strange behavior she exhibited began to grow as well.

In one particularly chilling incident, a mutual friend of Annaliese and Peter, named Anna Lippert, witnessed something unforgettable. In July of 1975, Anna, Annaliese, and Peter were casually chatting in Annaliese's dorm room when, without warning, Annaliese's face twisted into a demonic expression. Her entire body became rigid, as if catatonic. Shocked and terrified, Anna turned to Peter and asked what was happening.

Peter simply replied, "It's the demons. She's under possession."

Not knowing what else to do, the two prayed with Michel, but it took an hour and a half for the episode to end.

Following this happening, it became clear that Annaliese could no longer be by herself and attend school. The pair reached out to her parents, and they moved the young woman back home to Klingenburg several days later. Upon arriving, Annaliese was able to start eating again, but her other problems continued unabated. If anything, they worsened greatly in a very short period of time.

During a phone call between Father Alt and Michel's mother, the two were frequently interrupted by the horrendous screams of Annaliese from her room, screaming obscenities and overall being abhorrent.

Father Alt would ask a fellow priest closer to Annaliese to assist him in aiding her spiritual battle, a man named Father Roth. Upon reaching out to the family to arrange his meeting with them, Father Roth was surprised when Annaliese's mother answered the phone and said, "Father Roth?" The two had never met before, nor had she been informed by Father Alt of his call.

Bewildered, he said, "Yes that's me," and was then informed that Annaliese said they would send him. That right there to the priest was an indication of the demonic.

He arrived a week later. Upon entering the house, he heard the girl scream from her room up above. A horrible burning stench, like dung and sulfur, filled the living room he and Mrs. Michel chatted in. Trying to find the source of the scent, he thoroughly checked the house, including the exterior. He could not find an explainable origin. Mrs. Michel informed him Annaliese had been in the living room roughly twenty minutes prior.

Stepping outside to avoid the smell, the two spoke further, where Father Roth would be informed of Annaliese's outbursts of rage and generally bizarre behavior. The family begged him to pray over her. To this he agreed.

Reluctantly walking upstairs to Annaliese's room for the first time, he couldn't help but notice the abnormal number of dead bugs lining the hallway. Upon opening the door, he was besieged by the girl. She began cursing him, screaming at the top of her lungs, telling him not to dare take the crucifix out of his pocket, which he had not told anyone he was carrying.

She ran out of the bed and up to his face, stopping abruptly an inch or two away, frozen in place. Her eyes blackened and she said, "Oh priest, you may try."

She then collapsed to the floor in a catatonic state.

This was more than enough for Father Roth to rush to arrange a meeting with Father Alt to discuss what had taken place. Within days, the two met in person, during which Father Roth explained that he had no doubts the girl was being troubled by demons. That he had no doubt it was indeed the real deal.

The two sought to move forward asking for formal permission to begin the exorcism process. During the wait for final approval over the course of the next year, a web of disgust and horror was woven as her family, Peter, and the priests experienced a plethora of horrendous manifestations at the hands of Annaliese.

Following Father Roth's initial visit, Annaliese became extremely restless, at most sleeping one or two hours a night. She ran through the house on all fours, barking and screaming like an animal. She was visibly forcibly moved by something no one could see. During her prayers, which were constant at this point, she would do knee busters – standing up only to aggressively drop to her knees at the expense of her kneecaps, no matter how awfully injured they were. The joints became swollen and ulcerated, but she persisted.

She screamed constantly, the incessant yelling echoing all through the walls, day and night, rising and falling like waves against a rocky shore. She trembled and twitched, becoming rigid and catatonic, having to be moved back into her bed by her family.

Amidst her escalating madness, and now weighing barely a hundred pounds, she began to display superhuman strength. Peter witnessed her crush an apple with one frail hand and hurl her sister Roswitha across the room like a rag doll. She also began to smash her face into walls and floors, leading to her mother placing pillows all around in an effort to stop her from injuring herself.

With the Michel family's world turning upside down, Annaliese stopped eating and drinking altogether – normal food that is. She began stuffing the overabundance of insects into her mouth, eating roaches, hordes of flies, and spiders. Her behavior became more unhinged; she began to chew on coal and rocks which ultimately broke several of her teeth. She would urinate on the floor and lick it up.

Among the chaos, her family began to experience what can only be described as demonic manifestations. Clouds of flies would spontaneously appear and dissipate just as rapidly all over their home, even in winter. Shadowy figures ran throughout their home, with no visible source.

As Annaliese raged on, her family and Peter took to alternating two-hour shifts to try and take care of her, attempting to prevent her from further inflicting wounds on herself. Josef knew with how dire circumstances were, they could not continue this way. Out of desperation, he telegraphed Father Alt, begging him for assistance.

Father Alt, who had been in touch with his superiors at the church, informed him he believed Annaliese should be admitted to a psychiatric hospital for evaluation. However, this changed after he passed on the slew of details Josef shared with him about the dramatic worsening of Annaliese's behavior and overall condition to a fellow priest by the name of Father Rodewyk.

Father Rodewyk agreed to go and see the girl for himself. Upon entering the Michel house, Josef introduced him to

Annaliese, walking her into the living room himself, for she had become violent towards the family.

Sitting down beside her, Father Rodewyk asked, "What is your name?"

In a very low, altered voice that was not her own, she said, "Judas."

Over the course of the next several hours, the father was able to have a normal conversation with Annaliese, after the demonic force receded. She had no recollection of what happened while she was under outside influence.

Towards the end of the meeting, she slapped the father across his face, then stood up and walked towards the piano. She began playing it as if nothing had happened.

Father Rodewyk informed the family he would indeed help her and support them, that he ultimately believed Annaliese to be possessed and would seek action immediately.

After much deliberation, the church finally came around. A priest by the name of Father Renz, an experienced exorcist, was tasked with the ritual. On a cold, rainy day it began – September 24th, 1975.

After discussing the plan with her family, he proceeded up the stairs and walked into the viper's den that was Annaliese's room. He was joined by Josef, Peter, and a volunteer of the congregation who wanted to assist.

At first, all was silent. Annaliese, or rather, the demons were not engaging Father Renz.

When he began the ritual, however, he sprinkled holy water on Annaliese, causing her to scream and shake. She started biting the men who were . holding her and screamed, lunging at the priest in a feverish attempt to attack him. It took all three men to hold her down.

The events were recorded in an entry in Father Renz's diary. He went on to say she would sound like a man, speak Latin, and eventually be reduced to a catatonic state. Knowing he had a long battle ahead of him, the priest was saddened by the first ritual's lack of efficacy.

He left for the night, returning four days later on the evening of September 28th. He brought a recorder with him in hopes of providing a record for future study at the church. Due to this decision, we now have some of the disturbing audio available to us.

Annaliese repeated the chaotic behavior she exhibited within the first exorcism and the devil residing within her began to rebut the priest in Latin, as well as German. Although familiar with the Latin language, Annaliese was not fluent enough to form rebuttals in such a timely manner.

Upon asking why he tormented the girl, it replied, "She was cursed before she was born," by a woman, a neighbor of her mother in Lieblfing. Annaliese's parents and Peter attempted to check the story out later, but the woman had since died.

This exorcism lasted for hours and ended with a haunting sentence from Annaliese: *"Auf Ewigkiet*

*Verdammt O-oh."* Which in English means, *"Damned for all eternity."*

She promptly curled back up into a catatonic state, still as a statue.

There are only scant further details based on diary entries, interviews, and audio recordings, but this continued for months. Annaliese would undergo 67 exorcisms in total.

She revealed she was possessed by five demons: Cain, Judas, Nero, Fleischmann, and Lucifer, the devil in the flesh.

- Cain is known from the Bible as the first murderer, the originator of violence.
- Judas, as in Judas Iscariot – the man who betrayed Jesus Christ.
- Nero, the crazed Roman emperor who tortured Christians for his own enjoyment.
- Fleischmann who was a disgraced local priest.
- And finally, Lucifer, the prince of darkness himself.

Annaliese's physical condition declined due to not being able to eat, self-inflicted injuries, and psychosis resulting from lack of sleep. These finally took their toll. She informed Father Renz on June 30th, at the end of what would be their final exorcism, that she had spoken with the Virgin Mary. She agreed to stay on earth and suffer through the demons to prove to people who didn't believe in God that the devil was very real. She then asked for absolution, which the father granted her.

That night, she went silent for the first time since all of these horrifying episodes began. The following morning, around 7am on July 1, 1976, she was found dead.

All of the exorcisms and attempts to drive the demons out had failed.

Annaliese Michel had gone from a shy but happy girl with her whole life ahead of her to an emaciated shell of herself. Just how did we get here? Was it malpractice? Was she mentally ill? Or was it truly demonic hands that snuffed her life out?

After multiple calls made by her grieving family, a man named Dr. Kehler performed the postmortem examination. It's important to note the resulting information. Her cause of death was determined to be starvation, and possibly aggravated and tremendous physical exertion in the final weeks of her life. He found her inner organs were surprisingly healthy and not damaged, including her brain, which showed no signs of epilepsy, not even on a microscopic level. Curiouser still, no bruising, bed sores, or ulcerations were found on her skin.

In the ensuing aftermath, the priest was arrested and charged with negligent homicide along with Josef and Anna. The trial and case overall would become a highly debated issue among the German people at the time. Some were convinced she died at the hands of the devil. Others believed it was the fault of malpractice on behalf of the priests and her parents. The trial lasted for months, with doctors, lawyers, and witnesses weighing in with their opinions.

After much heated debate, Michel's parent's and the priests involved were charged with negligent homicide and sentenced to 6 months in prison. The 6 months ultimately would be reduced to 3 years of probation, as well as a fine given the unique circumstances of the case.

The church drew a ton of heat as a result of the case and, several years later, retracted the confirmation that she was indeed possessed.

Annaliese Michel was buried under hurried circumstances and as a result of this, as well as multiple religious people stating that they had experienced visions of her body untouched by decay. She was exhumed almost two years later to be buried in a nicer coffin. Her family and friends were discouraged from viewing her remains because they were consistent with a corpse of that age.

Her case went on to achieve worldwide notoriety and forced the Catholic church to all but never issue sanctioned exorcisms.

On June 6, 2013, the home in which her exorcisms took place mysteriously caught fire and burned to the ground. Police suspected arson, but many locals believed it was a result of what had taken place there.

Decades after her death, her story went on to inspire multiple films and books, The Exorcism of Emily Rose being the most popular and accurate, with some liberties to the original story. Of the many books, the best and most utilized resource of them for me has been *The Exorcism of Annaliese Michel* by Felicitas D. Goodman. All, and I mean *all*, the details you could ever want about the entire case are available within that book.

Overall, Annaliese's case continues to be both terrifying and shrouded in mystery. Was she demonically possessed or incredibly mentally ill? Did her priests and parents genuinely help her in being freed from Satan's grasp or did they contribute to the end of her life accidentally? Ultimately, the choice is yours to make. Regardless of the cause, I am truly glad that her suffering is over and now she can hopefully rest in peace.

# CHAPTER 9
## THE LONG ISLAND TERROR

Can rebuilding your life lead to unforeseen destruction? Could it awaken an ancient evil? After a family loses their father in a devastating fire, the widow and her two children seek a fresh start. But when they move into what was meant to be a new beginning, they soon realize they are not the only ones living there. As dark entities emerge from the walls, intent on claiming their souls, the question becomes: will they survive, or will they be consumed by the darkness that surrounds them?

All events occurred between 2005 and 2011 in Long Island, NY

---

Our story begins with a building engulfed in flames in the Bronx, New York. Firefighters, battling the inferno, become trapped on the top floor of the four-story complex. Tragically, all six are forced to make an impossible choice: jump or succumb to the flames. Some survive, while others do not. Lieutenant Curtis Meyran of Battalion 26, the husband of Jeanette Meyran, was among those who did not make it. Curt was more than just a firefighter; he was a devoted family man, a loving husband, and father of two. His sudden and tragic death left a deep, devastating impact on everyone who knew him.

The heartbreaking events shattered any semblance of the future Jeanette had envisioned. After the tragedy, she had to break the devastating news to her two daughters that they would never see their father again. The girls were inconsolable. To make matters worse, in the days following the public announcement, their home was besieged by the media. There was no care, no compassion —just a relentless pursuit for a quote and a photograph to sell the latest headline.

The harassment was constant during this time. As Jeanette contemplated how to navigate the crisis, she began to wonder if she should find a small place somewhere for her and the girls to escape to—a place where they could start over and begin fresh. One afternoon, with snow still melting outside, she took the girls for a drive and seemingly stumbled upon a deal that felt like an answer to her prayers.

Located outside the city, on a rare acre of land, stood a rather large home. It needed some work, but Jeanette felt confident she could make it happen. From the moment she laid eyes on it, she knew this was the one. It could be a way to give her daughters and herself a new life. Seizing the opportunity, she made an offer, and to her amazement, it was accepted. Within a month, the Meyrans moved from the home that Curtis had built to a new house, a fresh start outside the city.

With each bag and box of belongings transferred, they felt as if they were getting closer to the peace they all desperately wanted. The home, as mentioned, needed some restoration, but with Curtis having been a firefighter, his brothers in service took it upon themselves to look out for his family. With all the manpower, the work was expected to be completed within a couple of weeks. However, the restoration of the home would soon be followed by unexpected devastation.

As construction continued in an unfamiliar area, valuable tools were occasionally left lying around, raising concerns about both their safety and security. Jen decided to install security cameras to monitor the property. They installed a total of seven cameras around the house. On the first night the cameras were operational, Jen was curious to see what they could detect. Being new to this technology, she sat in the living room with her computer, tuning in to what was happening outside her walls.

It was nighttime, and the cameras had switched to night vision mode, displaying everything in black and white. As she clicked through the different camera feeds, the evening progressed without much activity—until she suddenly noticed a man standing in the middle of one frame, staring directly at the house. Given the camera quality at the time, she didn't panic, thinking perhaps her eyes were playing tricks on her. Still, to be safe, she ensured that the house was completely secure and eventually managed to relax enough to try to get some sleep.

As an icy wind blows outside and a light snow gently coats the earth, Jeanette and her two girls lay in their beds. Her mother and sister are asleep, as far as she knows, but Angela is particularly restless. She can't seem to sleep, tossing and turning with an uneasy feeling in the pit of her stomach. As she struggles to settle down in her room, she is suddenly interrupted by a strange banging sound. Sitting up to listen, she hears it again. However, these thumps or knocks seem to be coming from inside the walls.

Turning on her lamp and getting out of bed, Angela begins to investigate as the noises grow louder. Meanwhile, unbeknownst to her, her younger sister Danine is awakened by the sound of someone banging on the outside of her closed bedroom door. She calls out but is met with nothing but silence.

Finding this strange and confused after being abruptly woken from a deep sleep, the young girl cautiously gets out of bed and slowly makes her way to the door. As she turns the knob and peers through the opening, she swings the door wide open, only to find an empty hallway leading to her sister's room across the way.

At the same time, Angela is still investigating the sounds coming from within the walls of her room. The banging has grown more rhythmic and aggressive, as if someone

—or something—is desperately trying to get her attention. The sounds seem to move around the room, and in an attempt to pinpoint their origin, she walks over to the wall beside her dresser and slowly presses her ear against it to listen. Suddenly, the banging intensifies, almost as if it has found her. Eyes wide with fear, she quickly steps back from the wall as the mysterious sound continues.

Meanwhile, Danine, unaware of her sister's ordeal, closes her door and sits back on her bed. Almost immediately, the knocking starts again, but this time it shakes her entire door. Terrified, she quickly hides under her covers. As the night wears on, the two sisters are gripped with fear, and needless to say, they get little rest. The unsettling activities finally seem to cease at dawn.

The next morning, as their mom serves them breakfast, she notices that her two girls look utterly exhausted.

When Jeanette asks what's going on with them, she is soon met with a barrage of questions: Was she the one knocking on the walls or their doors? Was she walking around the house all night? Confused, Jeanette explains that she hadn't heard anything during the night. She attributes their experiences to the girls adjusting to the emotions of everything—the move, the new environment. She hopes that with time, they will warm up to the house and all will be well. The girls, feeling that their mom might not believe them, hold back from fully expressing their fear. Instead, they continue eating their breakfast and try to steer the conversation to another topic.

As the girls go about their day, Jen decides to go upstairs to investigate their rooms but finds nothing out of the ordinary. The renovations continue, and soon the firemen find themselves working in the basement of the house. Described as unique and cluttered with debris, they set to work demolishing old boards and clearing things out.

Meanwhile, the girls explore the backyard. They've never seen an area so large, and despite the freezing weather, they decide to venture out. However, they start noticing some strange things about their new playground. The first thing that catches their attention are strange symbols carved into several trees on the property. Unsure of what to make of it, they let their imaginations run wild and decide to create a map to help them hide things. As they continue exploring, they make another, even stranger discovery: several chipped bones tied together with a lace-like material, dangling from a low-hanging branch of one of the trees. Though they find it really odd, they are unsure what to make of it, so they continue playing.

As the firefighters remove debris and old demolition waste from the basement, they soon make a startling discovery. Beneath the old floorboards, etched into the concrete below, is an inverted pentagram. They quickly call Jen to take a look. Curious about what it might be, she comes down and sees it for the first time. As she gazes at it, a wave of nausea washes over her. She instructs the men to cover it back up, not wanting her girls to see it. The men agree to lay new concrete over it, ensuring her daughters will never know it was there.

Meanwhile, the girls, still playing outside in their winter wonderland, make yet another discovery. They stumble upon several stars made out of bones scattered on the ground. Thinking it's part of some game, they innocently incorporate them into their play. Oh, the innocence of children.

Several days later, Jen returns to work, leaving Angela in charge of her younger sister. Angela is also tasked with cleaning up the house. As she moves through the house, checking off her list, she feels an unsettling presence, as if she's not alone. She keeps glancing over her shoulder, but nothing seems to be there. Just as she turns back to her cleaning, she hears an ear-shattering noise. Her eyes dart to the origin of the sound, and she's horrified by what she sees. The entire kitchen has been turned upside down—pans and dishes are strewn out of their cabinets, and silverware that was once neatly inside drawers is now scattered everywhere. Terrified and not knowing what else to do, she screams and flees, running upstairs to her room.

When Jen arrives home from work, she walks into an eerily quiet house. In her own words, "When I walked inside, everything was very quiet. I glanced into the kitchen, and every cabinet, every drawer was emptied. The place looked like it had been ransacked. I called out for Angela but got no response."

Assuming her daughter might have had a tantrum, Jen begins searching for Angela after not receiving an answer. Rushing upstairs, she finds her daughter holding a stuffed animal and staring blankly ahead. When confronted, Angela tells her mother what happened, and thankfully, Jen believes her. She recognizes the sincerity in her child's eyes and voice.

The following day, while both children are out, Jen greets a few workers in the basement who are putting the finishing touches on the renovation. One of them has found something while working—a bundle of old-looking papers tied together with some kind of white lace. Handing the papers to Jen, she begins to unfurl them. The first date on the pages goes back to 1927, the year the home was originally built.

As she scours the pages for more information, Jen realizes that the diary seems to have been written by a young girl, perhaps the daughter of someone who once lived in the house. As she continues reading, she learns that the girl's name was Christina, and her story would take a very dark turn.

Christina began to describe how her father would harm animals on a star in the basement, and as the pages went on, the descriptions grew darker and more graphic. He would use the animals' blood to paint shapes on the walls.

Disturbed by what she had just read, Jen decided that no one else needed to know about what had happened in the house. If the diary was true, the previous occupants were deeply troubled, and Jen, now living there, wanted to wash her hands of their actions and pretend that nothing had ever happened in the place she and her children now called home. Who could blame her? But some things don't stay buried.

The following day, as Jen is cleaning, she is suddenly startled by a massive boom that shakes the entire house. Shocked by the unexpected noise, she realizes it's coming from the basement below. Fearing that something might have exploded, she apprehensively makes her way to the basement door. With a flashlight in hand, she slowly begins her descent down the stairs. Once she reaches the concrete floor, she scans the room for any signs of what might have caused the commotion. As she steps forward and peers around, her flashlight suddenly dies. Jen then begins to feel as if the oxygen in the room is being consumed rapidly, and an overwhelming sense of dread overtakes her. She races up the stairs as fast as she can, slamming the door behind her, feeling as if she had just been in the presence of pure evil.

Still concerned and unsure whether the noise had something to do with the plumbing or another issue, Jen knows she needs to address the potential cause. However, too frightened to continue, she decides to put it on the back burner, at least for now.

Later that night, after feeding the family dinner, Jen is busy cleaning up while Angela is in her room and Danine is taking a shower. As Angela sits on her bed reading a magazine, she suddenly begins to hear the faintest of whispers. It sounds like multiple voices whispering at once from a distance. Perplexed, she gets up and tries to find the source of these mysterious whispers. As she steps toward her door, the whispers grow louder, making it possible to discern some of the conversation. It seems to be a secretive exchange between two people.

Convinced the voices are just outside her door, Angela throws it open, only to find nothing. As she does, the whispers abruptly stop. More confused than ever, she closes the door and heads back to her bed, but the whispers start again. Returning to the door, she listens closely and this time hears her sister's name mentioned in the secret conversation.

Meanwhile, as Angela experiences this unsettling event, Danine, who is showering, begins to have her own terrifying encounter. Feeling as if she's being watched but trying to shake off the sensation, she hurries to finish her shower. When she hears the door creak open, it puts her on edge. Calling out to the steam-tinted glass, she asks if it's her mother or Angela who entered the bathroom. What she sees next is horrifying: through the blur of the steam, she makes out the silhouette of a large creature with pointed ears and grotesque features. Terrified, Danine cowers in the corner of the shower, screaming for her mother.

Across the hallway upstairs, Angela, who had overheard what sounded like two people whispering about her sister, hears Danine's cries and immediately rushes toward her bathroom. At the same time, Jen, startled by the screams, also runs upstairs. They try to open the bathroom door, but it won't budge—it's seemingly locked from the inside. As they frantically attempt to get inside to save Danine, she continues to scream as the creature presses its face and hands against the glass, revealing black, rotting skin, yellow eyes, and sharp teeth.

Finally, the door swings open, as if the unseen force holding it shut has suddenly vanished. Rushing inside to help Danine, they find her trembling with the shower still running. Jen quickly turns off the water and wraps a towel around her, then hurries them all out of the bathroom. But as they stand in the hallway, every door in the house that was open slams shut on its own. Simultaneously, a dark, demonic chanting fills the house, growing louder and more oppressive, as if some abomination from their worst nightmares is inching closer. The fear among them intensifies as they run to Jen's bedroom, throwing open the door and rushing inside before slamming it shut behind them to barricade themselves from whatever is approaching.

Jen holds the door shut, bracing herself in case the entity tries to break in. All three are in hysterical tears, crying out for their father—Jen's husband, their lost protector. Something begins slamming against the door, as if trying to break it down. As the noise outside intensifies, they desperately call out for Curtis. Although they don't feel his presence, just as quickly as it all began, the chaos outside the door and the evil presence abruptly stop.

The following day, desperate to talk to someone but afraid of being judged as crazy, Jen contemplates who she could confide in. Her husband's longtime friend, Tony, had been there for her and the girls since the tragedy occurred. If anyone would believe her, it would be him. So, she gives him a call, and within half an hour, he arrives at the house. After sitting down together at the kitchen table, Jen explains everything to him—from the discovery of the pentagram in the basement to the strange occurrences they've been experiencing, especially what happened the night before.

After hearing Jen's account, Tony decides to go into the basement to take a look around. She guides him to the door but refuses to go down with him. Handed a flashlight, Tony descends the stairs alone. In his own words, "I didn't fear much in life, but while in the basement, I couldn't shake the feeling that something was watching me. It felt like there was an oppressive atmosphere, making it hard to breathe. I wanted to get out of there as soon as possible."

Suddenly, he is spooked by the sound of a door rattling. As he approaches it, the rattling continues, further unnerving him. Not wanting to delay the inevitable, Tony throws the door open, only to find nothing physically there. Already on edge, he steps outside the small room the door concealed, and as soon as he does, the door slams shut behind him. This final unsettling event convinces Tony it's time to get the hell out of there. Despite his 25 years as a corrections officer, during which he feared very little, what he experienced in that basement rattled him to the core. He explains what happened to Jen but decides to leave shortly after the ordeal.

Moving forward, in an attempt to comfort one another, they decided that whenever someone was showering, another person would wait outside the bathroom door to keep them company in case anything happened. With all their money tied up in the house, Jen was desperate to find a solution. Although not very religious, she decided to call the Catholic Church for help based on what she knew.

The following day, a priest arrived to assess the situation and perform a blessing for the family. He not only confirmed that there was something evil within the home but also strategized with Jen on how to try and rid the house of whatever was haunting it. He conducted a blessing of the home and advised Jen to find her inner faith, suggesting that she conduct regular blessings herself. He provided her with gallons of holy water, which she placed in spray bottles to cover every square inch of the home during these blessings.

One night, after Jen performed a blessing, Angela, who had become fairly withdrawn due to the stress and trauma of their situation, went outside to the swing set in their backyard. Since it was nighttime, Jen decided to keep an eye on her using the cameras she had installed. As Angela quietly swung, deep in thought, it soon became apparent that she was not alone. Occasionally glancing at the laptop screen where the cameras were being monitored, Jen noticed something strange: several dark, hooded figures had suddenly appeared, surrounding Angela. With her heart pounding, Jen rushed as fast as she could toward the back door and her daughter.

Unaware of the figures her mother had seen, Angela continued swinging at a steady, normal pace. Suddenly, she was violently thrust out of the seat, slamming into the snow-packed ground with tremendous force. Upon impact, she heard a horrendous crack. Crying out in pain for her mother, Angela was met by Jen, who immediately began throwing holy water around them, screaming and cursing the figures that had hurt her daughter. Scrambling to get Angela to their vehicle, Jen drove her straight to the hospital, where they quickly discovered that Angela's foot and ankle were shattered.

The following morning, after returning from the hospital, Angela, now wearing a boot on her broken ankle, was forced to stay in bed, further isolating her and keeping her confined to the house. While things seemed relatively calm during the day, the house came alive after sunset.

One night, while incapacitated in her room and with Jen out running errands with her sister, Angela lay alone on her bed. It was lightly snowing outside, and moonlight peeked through her blinds. Suddenly, she heard a faint knocking noise coming from her closet. Glancing over, she noticed her mirror looked strange, almost liquid. Then she saw something that filled her with absolute terror—a charred, black, clawed hand began emerging from the mirror, slowly and menacingly inching out further.

Terrified, Angela began to scream, unable to run away—not only because her foot was broken, but also because the mirror was directly in front of her door. Desperate, she threw herself onto the floor and rolled under her bed, pressing herself as far back against the wall as possible. The stench of decay filled the room as the creature slowly emerged from the mirror. From her hiding spot, Angela could see only the gnarled feet of the entity as it stepped toward the bed. Grasping the home phone, she frantically began dialing her mother's number.

On the other end of the line, Jen picks up. She had been grocery shopping, but upon hearing her daughter's screams, she abandons everything and immediately rushes toward the house, though she is 45 minutes away. Pleading with Angela to pray as she speeds on the slick roads, Jen suddenly hears a horrendous scream—something unearthly, unlike anything she had ever heard before—and then the phone call abruptly drops. Angela, who had been reciting the Hail Mary while on the phone with her mother, was suddenly face-to-face with the demon.

After rushing home as fast as she could, Jen arrives to find the house dark and eerily silent. All the lights are off, and she hears nothing. Running up the stairs to Angela's room, she finds it empty. With tears streaming down her face, she fears the worst—until she hears the faintest whimper coming from under the bed. It's Angela, so weak and fragile that Jen has to drag her out. With both of her girls now in her room, Jen frantically searches online for help, knowing that they deserve a future, but fearing that one of them may end up hurt again—or worse—if things continue this way.

During her research, she finds the contact information for a paranormal investigator named Liz. Desperate, she calls the number at 3 a.m. Liz answers, and after hearing Jen's harrowing story, she decides to help. Having researched the paranormal for over 15 years, Liz believes she must conduct a cleansing of the home. Within several hours, just after daybreak, Liz arrives, accompanied by her friend and colleague, Dawn, a psychic medium.

As soon as Liz and Dawn greet Jen at her door and step inside, Dawn begins receiving flashes of the past. She quickly senses that many rituals were conducted within the home, specifically in the basement—details she hadn't been told beforehand. Dawn believes these rituals were performed by dark cults that communicated with and conjured demonic entities, and that the recent renovations disturbed the energies within the house. After discussing her impressions, the women decide to lay a circle of salt around the property, intending to create a barrier that no spirit can cross, either in or out. For Jen, this felt like the beginning of the final showdown with the malevolent forces tormenting her family.

After laying the salt circle while praying, they head back inside and light several bundles of sage. Together, they move from room to room, blessing and cleansing each space, allowing the sage smoke to fill the air. Slowly but surely, they work through the entire house until they reach the basement—the apparent epicenter of the demonic activity. Together, they descend the stairs, their prayers filling the sage-saturated air.

As they continue through the basement, they begin to hear the same unsettling noises Jen and her children had previously encountered—loud chants in a language they couldn't understand. With each flick of holy water and each prayer, they soon start to hear screams accompanying the chanting, the entire episode gradually reaching a crescendo. Finally, they approach the last space yet to be cleansed: the room behind the door where Tony had his terrifying experience. Once again, the door begins to violently shake.

Determined to end this once and for all, they threw the door open, allowing the sage smoke to infiltrate the last untouched air of the home. As they prayed and cast holy water into the space, flames suddenly erupted from the floor, revealing a screaming, charred demonic figure. But this horrifying vision lasted only for the briefest moment. Almost as soon as the women's screams began, the fire extinguished, and the long battle with this horrendous demon was finally over.

The cleansing conducted by Liz and Dawn was indeed successful. Jen and her daughters still live in the home to this day. This experience serves as a reminder that the evil forces lurking just beyond the veil of our world have nothing but contempt for us. No tragedy or sorrow is enough to be left alone; instead, these forces exploit such vulnerabilities to weaken, attack, and consume those most susceptible. Yet, this family banded together and overcame the terror of the demonic, proving that love truly does conquer hate.

I want to acknowledge the incredible strength shown by everyone involved, especially Jen, Angela, and Danine. Not only did they endure the heartache of losing Curtis, but they also faced the terror of this horrendous haunting. They pressed on, fought for their home and their lives, and proved themselves to be remarkably strong and brave. I have nothing but the utmost respect for them. I also hope that, with the information I found, I have done their story justice in my retelling.

# CHAPTER 10
## THE EXORCISM OF ROLAND DOE

Considered to be one of the most terrifying films of all time, the movie The Exorcist paralyzed the masses upon its release and brought the devil home to millions of people. Although the horror and special effects enhanced the story being portrayed, what if I told you the story itself was inspired by a true story of demonic possession?

When a young boy loses his beloved aunt, he starts to dabble with the occult and makes contact with the other side, but what he contacts isn't what he bargained for. What follows not only terrified a family but, by proxy, thousands of people all over the world. This is the terrifying story of exorcism of Roland Doe and the demons that plagued him.

*Note: Roland Doe and Robbie Doe are aliases used to conceal the true identity of the individual/s involved.

Our story starts in 1949 in the small town of Cottage City, Maryland. A boy who we'll call Roland Doe was mourning the death of his beloved Aunt. Aunt Millie's passing was very sudden and the two had been extremely close. Millie was known for being an avid spiritualist, perhaps a new age person of her time, and was always very interested in things like spirits, the afterlife, and Ouija boards.

Seeing this activity, the young Roland became very interested as well and Aunt Millie taught him how to properly use a Ouija board to contact the other side. As Roland mourned her over the summer of 1948, he rediscovered the Ouija board that Aunt Millie had given him, tucked away in a trunk of belongings. In a moment of desperation, he laid the board on a nearby table and attempted to speak with Aunt Millie once again. Alas, despite his best efforts, no movement came from the board. It is this moment that is believed to be the catalyst for what would follow.

Just days after Roland used the Ouija board, things started happening, but not with the board itself. The entire family started hearing a steady, dripping sound with seemingly no origin. After this continued for about a week, they called in a plumber who ultimately found no evidence of any sort of pipe leak. Then the drips turned into thumps and scratches, both of which seemed to come from everywhere inside the walls.

The family tried to make sense of the activity, first suspecting mice. As they had with the potential leak situation, they had a well-known exterminator come out. He, too, found no evidence of any sort of infestation.

Over the next several months, things continued to escalate. Furniture began to move by itself, and other items were hurled across the room by an invisible force. A portrait of Jesus that hung on the wall began to rattle and shake as if it was being hit from behind.

The happenings continued to grow in intensity, leading to a crescendo. The force seemed to move out of the walls and into Roland's room, into his bed. One night, he was violently awakened to his bed shaking profusely. He screamed for his mother, who came in and experienced the terror with him, leaving both of them at a loss for words.

The family tried to decipher what was happening. They soon had Roland examined by a doctor and then a psychiatrist. Both of them concluded that the young man was very stressed out, but otherwise healthy.

Day after day the poor boy was being plagued by forces he couldn't see or defend himself against. Markings began to materialize on his body. The first markings spelled out the word:

*Booth's.*

Beyond frightened and trying to find a resolution, the family used the Ouija board to try and contact Millie.

They made contact with something. When the board began to interact with them on its own, the atmosphere of the room changed. They asked for the spirit to prove that it was real. It obliged by hurling a chair across the living room. This wasn't the only sign.

The following morning, long burning welts appeared on Roland's legs, just as the previous markings had. This time they spelled out:

*Saint Louis*

The family now had to consider the unthinkable – that their son was perhaps in the grip of something demonic. They quickly contacted their local Lutheran pastor, who came to the house to pray with the family. After he witnessed the marks appear on the young man's body, he suggested that the family contact the Catholic Church since they tended to deal with such matters.

The family tried to flee the area in hopes that the activity would stay at the house. However, after relocating with a family member to a suburb of St. Louis, Missouri, the paranormal happenings continued.

Terrified and not knowing what else to do, the family reached out to Father Bowdern at the local Catholic parish. After a lengthy discussion, he wasn't convinced that the boy was possessed. Bowdern was a World War Two combat veteran and a hardened man, but very practical and religious. Not convinced but wanting to help ease the family's stress, he agreed to pray over the boy.

In due time he arrived at the house with a fellow priest by the name of Raymond Bishop. After meeting Roland, they all decided to pray together. To the priest's great surprise, as soon as the first several sentences of prayer were uttered, the boy began to scream that his chest was burning. Upon opening the boy's shirt, they saw red cuts begin to appear in the boy's skin. Scared, the priest began to pray over the boy more intensely, lasting from about 11 p.m. to 6 a.m. At the conclusion of this session, Roland finally fell into a restful sleep.

After explaining to the family their thoughts on what could be taking place, they decided that they would convene among themselves. As they tried to decide how to move forward to better assist Roland and his family, the priests returned to their homes and then met the following morning. It was here that both men decided that they were dealing with the real deal. Together, they made the decision to pursue an exorcism.

Father Bowdern, as senior priest, reached out to the Archbishop of Saint Louis to ask permission to perform the rights of exorcism, which he was granted under one request. That request was that he provided day to day account for the church, to which he agreed. Each segment of the story from here on out is written with excerpts of what the priest documented during his experiences.

Father Bowdern and Father Bishop returned to the residence a month later. As they prepared themselves, they entered Roland's frigid bedroom and began the ritual. The boy began to violently act out. With the help of the boy's father, subduing him, it continued. It would be written out that the boy's blows were beyond that of his age each punch had the strength of one or more grown men behind it. Father Bishop found this out the hard way mid prayer; Roland managed to break loose from his father and punch the priest in the face. It would later be discovered that he broke his nose.

Following the aftermath of this first night, all seemed calm for the first time in a long time. The boy did not act out, but rather was unconscious and just peacefully slept. They thought perhaps the prayers were beginning to work. That was until the priests left. Almost as quickly as their feet crossed the threshold of the residence, the boy began to yell and scream at the top of his lungs. This belligerent rage lasted for hours.

At the desperation of the parents, once they were able to recontact them, both priests returned as quickly as they could. With the assistance of both the boy's father and now mother, they had no other choice but to continue the ritual. For approximately four hours, Roland screamed and contorted.

Suddenly, the boy began to lurch as if he was going to throw up. He quickly asked for the window near his bed to be opened, which the family did. Roland rushed to the window and vomited a thick, black substance. Within minutes, he seemed to be his normal old self, for the first time in a long time. The boy seems to rest and for the first time, the family feels a true sense of relief.

The family and the priests knelt down thanked God, giving thanks for what seemed like a triumph of good over evil. But from *Rituale Romanum*, the Catholic rites of exorcism, sometimes the devil will leave the possessed person in peace to make it appear as if he is departed. The Exorcist must see through this with the power of God and realize this trap.

Come 2 a.m., an uneasy quiet filled the house. The priests had been gone for several hours. Then suddenly, Roland's screams began to fill the house – deep, guttural screams, as if something otherworldly was trying to break through his physical vessel.

There is no rest for the wicked, nor is there rest for the good. The priests were called back yet again by Roland's parents and arrived around 3:15am, shortly into the bewitching hour. They returned to Roland's bedside where he began taunting and screaming at the priests, an all too familiar happening at that point.

After several more hours of intense prayer, seemingly out of nowhere, the young man went catatonic around 6 a.m. He was frozen like a statue. For all intents and purposes, he appeared to be sleeping, but with his eyes wide open. The priests, not wanting to leave the home in case the devil decided to reappear yet again, took to visiting with the family for several more hours. They conserved what little energy they had left and it's a good thing they did; bizarre activity resumed with a vengeance at 8:30 am. Various knocking noises accompanied Roland's screaming, resuming the seemingly never-ending hell.

Yet again, the prayers resumed. There was more violence than ever before. Roland exerted strength beyond his normal capacity. He began barking and screaming in multiple octaves, as if there were two voices inside him. Amidst the chaos, his mother broke down and had to leave the room for her own sanity. The boy she was looking at she no longer recognized as her son.

Within due time, Roland went catatonic again. Following the event, Father Bowdern suggested the boy be sent away to a worthy place where the exorcism could continue. He needed an unfamiliar and sanctified place that would assist them in calling upon God to intervene in what was quickly appearing to be the most intense case of possession seen in a very long time. It would also put Roland away from his mother, no longer causing her further distress as well. They ultimately decided to send him to a hospital run by an order of Catholic monks not too far from his home or the church the priests operated as a crossroad of sorts.

Due to the strange occurrences and violent outbursts, Roland was placed in a private room on a private floor above the psychiatric ward, not only for his own protection but to keep him from scaring the other patients within the hospital walls. Father Bowdern returned the following evening with Father Bishop, along with the additional help of Father Halloran, who was a young seminarian, was tasked with the main job of restraining the boy during prayers. When things were calm, he would speak with Roland and keep his spirits up.

After the priests made their way to the top floor and entered Roland's room, Father Halloran began visiting with Roland and his father. Bowdern then blessed him with a small vial of holy water. He placed the vial on the dresser next to the bed. Just a few seconds after this, the vial flew across the room and smashed into the wall, shattering to pieces.

In a later interview, as the only surviving priest who witnessed the activity, Father Halloran stated, "That's how I knew we were dealing with the real deal. When that vial flew by itself across the room and smashed into the wall opposite the dresser it was placed on... You read about these kinds of things, but they never really happen."

Realizing that they needed to initiate battle with the darkness that resided within the young man known as Roland Doe, the ritual formally began yet again. The boy began screaming and cursing the priests. He also revealed one of the telltale signs of possession as things began to escalate. Father Halloran's mother had recently passed away. It was something Roland had no way of knowing, especially since the two had only met for the first time that very day. He looked over at Halloran with a dark and sinister smile across his face and said his mother said hello – that she was rotting within the depths of hell.

This both angered and scared the young priest, but also served as a distinguishing factor for him personally: there was indeed another entity inhabiting the body of the boy that sat within the room with them. Something dark and malevolent.

As many of you may or may not know, exorcism typically speaking isn't a one and done kind of situation. It can take months or even years to fully rid someone of one or several demonic entities, if at all. Roland's case was no different. The prayers continued until Roland again went catatonic and was laid peacefully back into his bed.

Wanting to take an aggressive stance to rid the boy as fast as they could, all three priests and Roland's father returned the following day. Roland, by this time, was so violent that all four men had a hard time holding him down.

Aside from the multiple voices and curses, he began spitting a foul-smelling liquid at them. The boy screamed that Father Halloran was hurting him as he was restraining him. The young priest loosened his grip and was instantly punched in the face, breaking his nose and leaving him a bloody mess. This concluded prayers for that day.

The ordeal for all those involved was quickly becoming an excruciating nightmare they couldn't wake up from. Every day, all day there was very little sign of progress. For the priests, the task was exhausting, soul draining, and at times faith breaking. Despite the discouraging signs, like any battle that has to reach an inevitable conclusion, the ritual continues.

With each exorcism, Roland became more violent, angrier, and also began to spontaneously urinate, on top of other abhorrent behavior. More objects begin to move more regularly as the paranormal manifestations continue.

On day eighteen of Roland being in the hospital, he asked for a pen and paper from the priests. Upon receiving it, he wrote, "I am the devil himself. And within ten days, I will give you a sign."

Shortly after writing this down, he began to scream as the Roman numeral ten carved itself into the skin on his chest. Witnessing this, Father Bowdern decided to baptize the boy to hopefully aid his crusade against the demons that plagued him. The following day, with the boy's permission, he performs a baptism, which seemed to calm Roland down. After just ten minutes, the boy returned to his fists, anger, and curses.

Night after night, the praying continued. And night after night, the boy was overwhelmed.

As the prayers began one night, Roland screamed and there carved on his chest was:

*EXIT*

Horrified, the priests continued on with their prayers. The devil seemed to be speaking through Roland's body, saying, "You need to say one more word, but you never say it.

After the night's end at the hospital, the priests were puzzled. They pondered this strange statement. As they read through the book of exorcism, they realized that Father Bowdern was forgetting to read the word Lord, time and time again. This not only frighten the men further, but also affirmed their suspicions.

The following night – an ice cold, rainy evening – the priests arrived at the facility. They could immediately sense that something wasn't right. From the parking lot, they saw the lights on Roland's floor flickering on and off, in different rooms. As they checked in at the front desk, the clerk broke down in tears, trying to explain that things were especially bad. She was terrified.

As they approached the boy's room, they noticed a strong sulfuric smell coming from inside. Unlike previous nights, as soon as they entered the room, Roland began cursing at them. This time he spoke in fluent Latin, a language he had never been exposed to prior to the exorcisms beginning, let alone one he could've been fluent in. He also had never displayed foreign tongues before.

After the priests began the ritual again, Roland stated that was their sign. Father Bowdern then commanded the spirit to prove itself. As the words left the priest's lips, the boy smiled and touched the priest's purple vestments that were draped over his shoulders. They promptly burst into hundreds of individual fibers. With their worst fears realized, the priest began to pray harder than they had ever prayed before.

During the struggle, Roland broke a bed spring and attempted to stab Father Bowdern. Thankfully the boy was restrained before he could do so. He thrashed, urinated and screamed in dual octaves. Five hours into the prayers that night, he began to exhibit another new and frightening behavior. Before everyone's eyes, Roland tilted his head back and slowly began to float up towards the ceiling. Before he could reach the ceiling, the men forced themselves to power through their fear and grab the boy, bringing him back down to the bed. New restraints were then placed, tethering him from further floating.

After seven grueling hours of fighting, praying, and nerve wracking spiritual warfare, the boy gasped and exclaimed that he saw Saint Michael the Archangel use a flaming sword to drive the devil away. The saint hit him and drove him back into the darkest abyss one could imagine.

With this, he fell silent and finally closed his eyes and fell asleep – truly and peacefully asleep.

After this long and arduous night, what began twenty-eight days prior seemed to have finally been worth it. Roland slowly but surely returned to normal and in fact went on to live a rather ordinary life.

The records of the events from those twenty-eight days somehow were leaked to the press and became an embarrassment for both the priests and the individual involved. Father Bowdern always regretted Roland's confidentiality being violated.

William Peter Blatty, who had heard about the case, became extremely intrigued and reached out to the priest to discuss it with him. When asking if the whole thing was real or not, he replied, "I had no doubt about it then, and I have no doubt about it now. What was in the room that night was the otherworldly source we call the Devil in the flesh." William Peter Blatty took his inspiration from the case and wrote the book, *The Exorcist*.

So was the possession case of Roland Doe a genuine one?

It had been considered one of the most substantial cases, if not the most substantial case, by the Catholic Church in the last 300 years. This is particularly regarding the existence of satanic forces and the existence of demonic possessions. To others, it was just an emotionally compromised adolescent who was acting out after the death of a close loved one.

If the case was indeed the real deal, that has far-reaching implications in and of itself. The existence of true evil also implies the existence of true good. With the on-screen adaptation of The Exorcist, these deep reaching questions were brought to thousands if not millions of people all over the world. It led to a wider impact than perhaps anticipated.

Regarding Roland Doe, I think a deeper moral of this story is that the occult is not only very real, speaking from personal experience, but it is not for the non-experienced or spiritually weak. You can never be truly sure of what you're communicating with. For the majority of people, I would say this: just don't dabble. It will greatly benefit you not to, because what you might speak with may just be your worst nightmare come to life.

---

Thank you for reading.
Want more *Stories From The Archives*?
Get Volume 2

# About the Author

Kody Richardson, widely recognized as Mystery Archives, is a content creator and full-time paranormal investigator. Since debuting his work in 2020, he has amassed over 21 million views on YouTube.

Beyond his investigative pursuits, Kody is passionate about music, performing both vocals and drums for various projects. He also enjoys lifting weights at the gym and caring for his beloved turtle and dog, Luna.